A Virtuous Woman Bible Journal

NISSA WILLIAMS

WestBow
PRESS
A DIVISION OF THOMAS NELSON
& ZONDERVAN

WestBow Press books may be ordered through booksellers or by contacting:

WestBow Press
A Division of Thomas Nelson & Zondervan
1663 Liberty Drive
Bloomington, IN 47403
www.westbowpress.com
1 (866) 928-1240

ISBN: 978-1-4908-7768-6 (sc)

Library of Congress Control Number: 2015906623

Print information available on the last page.

WestBow Press rev. date: 5/11/2015

Dedication

I dedicate this Bible Journal to my precious gifts from God: Tony, Chris, and Hailie Williams. To my parents, Wilson and Carolyn Shields, my grandparents, Berlin and Mattie Morrow and Lonnie and Nannie Law, my sisters, Commander Lani Law, Dr. Dana Law, Sandra Shields-Moultrie, (Larry), who has always believed in me when I didn't believe in myself. To my nephews Braelon Shields and Jerome Byrd, III. Last, but never least, the man of my heart, Kelvin Newsome. I thank God for you every day.

I would like to give a huge, "Thank You" to three churches who have supported me and my Bible Journal's through the years: New Zion Bible Way Church in Birmingham, AL, Apostle Joseph and Lady Hamilton, preside; Mount Zion Baptist Church in Springville, AL, Pastor Larry and Lady Sharna Adams, preside; ONEeighty Church in Springville, AL, Pastor Gresh and Kori Harbuck, preside; and my church family.

Thank you, Natasha Hurd, for all the help and support you have given me throughout the years and encouraging my God-given talent. I thank God for placing you into my life.

Foreword

by Kim Black

I have the pleasure of working with and having a friend in Nissa for many years. She has a passion for people and a true love for Christ. This Bible Journal a very good tool for notes from sermons or just your own study of the Bible. As we know, the Bible is your manual for life and everything you will face on a daily basis. Use this Journal to keep up with the good and bad times, mark the "Book-Chapter-Verse" to use to deal with the issues life has given you and will give you. Go back later and look through the Bible and the use of the Bible Journal to see how God has used His word to speak into you. I pray the work and time Nissa has put in this Bible Journal will help you as much as mine has helped me.

*Trust in the LORD with all your heart
and lean not on your own understanding;
in all your ways acknowledge him,
and he will direct your paths.*

Proverbs 3:5-6 (NIV)

*For I know the thoughts that I think towards
you, saith the LORD, thoughts of peace, and
not of evil, to give you an expected end.*

Jeremiah 29:11 (KJV)

THIS VIRTUOUS WOMAN
BIBLE JOURNAL BELONGS TO

GIVEN BY

GIVEN ON

CHAPTER

1	51	101
2	52	102
3	53	103
4	54	104
5	55	105
6	56	106
7	57	107
8	58	108
9	59	109
10	60	110
11	61	111
12	62	112
13	63	113
14	64	114
15	65	115
16	66	116
17	67	117
18	68	118
19	69	119
20	70	120
21	71	121
22	72	122
23	73	123
24	74	124
25	75	125
26	76	126
27	77	127
28	78	128
29	79	129
30	80	130
31	81	131
32	82	132
33	83	133
34	84	134
35	85	135
36	86	136
37	87	137
38	88	138
39	89	139
40	90	140
41	91	141
42	92	142
43	93	143
44	94	144
45	95	145
46	96	146
47	97	147
48	98	148
49	99	149
50	100	150

OLD TESTAMENT

GENESIS EXODUS LEVITICUS NUMBERS
DEUTERONOMY JOSHUA JUDGES RUTH ISAMUEL
IISAMUEL IKINGS IIKINGS ICHRONICLES
IICHRONICLES EZRA NEHEMIAH ESTHER JOB
PSALMS PROVERBS ECCLESIASTES SONG OF
SOLOMON ISAIAH JEREMIAH LAMENTATIONS
EZEKIEL DANIEL HOSEA JOEL AMOS
OBADIAH JONAH MICAH NAHUM HABAKKUK
ZEPHANIAH HAGGAI ZECHARIAH MALACHI

_____
_____
_____
_____
_____
_____
_____
_____
_____
_____
_____
_____

NEW TESTAMENT

MATTHEW MARK LUKE JOHN ACTS ROMANS
ICORINTHIANS IICORINTHIANS GALATIANS
EPHESIANS PHILIPPIANS COLOSSIANS
ITHESSALONIANS IITHESSALONIANS
ITIMOTHY IITIMOTHY TITUS PHILEMON
HEBREWS JAMES IPETER IIPETER IJOHN
IIJOHN IIIJOHN JUDE REVELATION

_____
_____
_____
_____
_____
_____
_____
_____
_____

VERSE

1	51	101	151
2	52	102	152
3	53	103	153
4	54	104	154
5	55	105	155
6	56	106	156
7	57	107	157
8	58	108	158
9	59	109	159
10	60	110	160
11	61	111	161
12	62	112	162
13	63	113	163
14	64	114	164
15	65	115	165
16	66	116	166
17	67	117	167
18	68	118	168
19	69	119	169
20	70	120	170
21	71	121	171
22	72	122	172
23	73	123	173
24	74	124	174
25	75	125	175
26	76	126	176
27	77	127	
28	78	128	
29	79	129	
30	80	130	
31	81	131	
32	82	132	
33	83	133	
34	84	134	
35	85	135	
36	86	136	
37	87	137	
38	88	138	
39	89	139	
40	90	140	
41	91	141	
42	92	142	
43	93	143	
44	94	144	
45	95	145	
46	96	146	
47	97	147	
48	98	148	
49	99	149	
50	100	150	

CHAPTER			OLD TESTAMENT	VERSE			
1	51	101		1	51	101	151
2	52	102	GENESIS EXODUS LEVITICUS NUMBERS	2	52	102	152
3	53	103	DEUTERONOMY JOSHUA JUDGES RUTH ISAMUEL	3	53	103	153
4	54	104	IISAMUEL IKINGS IIKINGS ICHRONICLES	4	54	104	154
5	55	105		5	55	105	155
6	56	106	IICHRONICLES EZRA NEHEMIAH ESTHER JOB	6	56	106	156
7	57	107	PSALMS PROVERBS ECCLESIASTES SONG OF	7	57	107	157
8	58	108	SOLOMON ISAIAH JEREMIAH LAMENTATIONS	8	58	108	158
9	59	109		9	59	109	159
10	60	110	EZEKIEL DANIEL HOSEA JOEL AMOS	10	60	110	160
11	61	111	OBADIAH JONAH MICAH NAHUM HABAKKUK	11	61	111	161
12	62	112	ZEPHANIAH HAGGAI ZECHARIAH MALACHI	12	62	112	162
13	63	113		13	63	113	163
14	64	114		14	64	114	164
15	65	115	_____	15	65	115	165
16	66	116	_____	16	66	116	166
17	67	117	_____	17	67	117	167
18	68	118	_____	18	68	118	168
19	69	119	_____	19	69	119	169
20	70	120	_____	20	70	120	170
21	71	121	_____	21	71	121	171
22	72	122	_____	22	72	122	172
23	73	123	_____	23	73	123	173
24	74	124	_____	24	74	124	174
25	75	125	_____	25	75	125	175
26	76	126	_____	26	76	126	176
27	77	127	_____	27	77	127	
28	78	128	_____	28	78	128	
29	79	129	_____	29	79	129	
30	80	130	_____	30	80	130	
31	81	131	_____	31	81	131	
32	82	132	_____	32	82	132	
33	83	133	_____	33	83	133	
34	84	134	_____	34	84	134	
35	85	135	_____	35	85	135	
36	86	136	_____	36	86	136	
37	87	137		37	87	137	
38	88	138		38	88	138	
39	89	139	NEW TESTAMENT	39	89	139	
40	90	140		40	90	140	
41	91	141	MATTHEW MARK LUKE JOHN ACTS ROMANS	41	91	141	
42	92	142	ICORINTHIANS IICORINTHIANS GALATIANS	42	92	142	
43	93	143	EPHESIANS PHILIPPIANS COLOSSIANS	43	93	143	
44	94	144	ITHESSALONIANS IITHESSALONIANS	44	94	144	
45	95	145	ITIMOTHY IITIMOTHY TITUS PHILEMON	45	95	145	
46	96	146	HEBREWS JAMES IPETER IIPETER IJOHN	46	96	146	
47	97	147	IIJOHN IIIJOHN JUDE REVELATION	47	97	147	
48	98	148		48	98	148	
49	99	149		49	99	149	
50	100	150		50	100	150	

NOTES

*Who can find a virtuous woman? for her price **is** far above rubies.*
-Proverbs 31:10 (KJV)

NOTES

The heart of her husband doth **safely** trust in her, so that he shall have no need of spoil.
**-Proverbs 31:11(KJV)**

REFLECTIONS

_____

_____

_____

_____

_____

_____

_____

_____

_____

_____

_____

_____

_____

_____

_____

_____

_____

_____

_____

_____

_____

_____

_____

_____

_____

_____

She will do him good and not evil all the days of her life.
-Proverbs 31:12 (KJV)

REFLECTIONS

She seeketh wool, and flax, and worketh willingly with her hands.
-Proverbs 31:13(KJV)

CHAPTER

1	51	101
2	52	102
3	53	103
4	54	104
5	55	105
6	56	106
7	57	107
8	58	108
9	59	109
10	60	110
11	61	111
12	62	112
13	63	113
14	64	114
15	65	115
16	66	116
17	67	117
18	68	118
19	69	119
20	70	120
21	71	121
22	72	122
23	73	123
24	74	124
25	75	125
26	76	126
27	77	127
28	78	128
29	79	129
30	80	130
31	81	131
32	82	132
33	83	133
34	84	134
35	85	135
36	86	136
37	87	137
38	88	138
39	89	139
40	90	140
41	91	141
42	92	142
43	93	143
44	94	144
45	95	145
46	96	146
47	97	147
48	98	148
49	99	149
50	100	150

OLD TESTAMENT

GENESIS EXODUS LEVITICUS NUMBERS
DEUTERONOMY JOSHUA JUDGES RUTH ISAMUEL
IISAMUEL IKINGS IIKINGS ICHRONICLES
IICHRONICLES EZRA NEHEMIAH ESTHER JOB
PSALMS PROVERBS ECCLESIASTES SONG OF
SOLOMON ISAIAH JEREMIAH LAMENTATIONS
EZEKIEL DANIEL HOSEA JOEL AMOS
OBADIAH JONAH MICAH NAHUM HABAKKUK
ZEPHANIAH HAGGAI ZECHARIAH MALACHI

_____

_____

_____

_____

_____

_____

_____

_____

_____

_____

_____

_____

_____

NEW TESTAMENT

MATTHEW MARK LUKE JOHN ACTS ROMANS
ICORINTHIANS IICORINTHIANS GALATIANS
EPHESIANS PHILIPPIANS COLOSSIANS
ITHESSALONIANS IITHESSALONIANS
ITIMOTHY IITIMOTHY TITUS PHILEMON
HEBREWS JAMES IPETER IIPETER IJOHN
IIJOHN IIIJOHN JUDE REVELATION

_____

_____

_____

_____

_____

_____

_____

_____

VERSE

1	51	101	151
2	52	102	152
3	53	103	153
4	54	104	154
5	55	105	155
6	56	106	156
7	57	107	157
8	58	108	158
9	59	109	159
10	60	110	160
11	61	111	161
12	62	112	162
13	63	113	163
14	64	114	164
15	65	115	165
16	66	116	166
17	67	117	167
18	68	118	168
19	69	119	169
20	70	120	170
21	71	121	171
22	72	122	172
23	73	123	173
24	74	124	174
25	75	125	175
26	76	126	176
27	77	127	
28	78	128	
29	79	129	
30	80	130	
31	81	131	
32	82	132	
33	83	133	
34	84	134	
35	85	135	
36	86	136	
37	87	137	
38	88	138	
39	89	139	
40	90	140	
41	91	141	
42	92	142	
43	93	143	
44	94	144	
45	95	145	
46	96	146	
47	97	147	
48	98	148	
49	99	149	
50	100	150	

CHAPTER			OLD TESTAMENT	VERSE			
1	51	101		1	51	101	151
2	52	102	GENESIS EXODUS LEVITICUS NUMBERS	2	52	102	152
3	53	103	DEUTERONOMY JOSHUA JUDGES RUTH ISAMUEL	3	53	103	153
4	54	104	IISAMUEL IKINGS IIKINGS ICHRONICLES	4	54	104	154
5	55	105		5	55	105	155
6	56	106	IICHRONICLES EZRA NEHEMIAH ESTHER JOB	6	56	106	156
7	57	107	PSALMS PROVERBS ECCLESIASTES SONG OF	7	57	107	157
8	58	108	SOLOMON ISAIAH JEREMIAH LAMENTATIONS	8	58	108	158
9	59	109		9	59	109	159
10	60	110	EZEKIEL DANIEL HOSEA JOEL AMOS	10	60	110	160
11	61	111	OBADIAH JONAH MICAH NAHUM HABAKKUK	11	61	111	161
12	62	112	ZEPHANIAH HAGGAI ZECHARIAH MALACHI	12	62	112	162
13	63	113		13	63	113	163
14	64	114	_____	14	64	114	164
15	65	115	_____	15	65	115	165
16	66	116	_____	16	66	116	166
17	67	117	_____	17	67	117	167
18	68	118	_____	18	68	118	168
19	69	119	_____	19	69	119	169
20	70	120	_____	20	70	120	170
21	71	121	_____	21	71	121	171
22	72	122	_____	22	72	122	172
23	73	123	_____	23	73	123	173
24	74	124	_____	24	74	124	174
25	75	125	_____	25	75	125	175
26	76	126	_____	26	76	126	176
27	77	127	_____	27	77	127	
28	78	128	_____	28	78	128	
29	79	129	_____	29	79	129	
30	80	130	_____	30	80	130	
31	81	131	_____	31	81	131	
32	82	132	_____	32	82	132	
33	83	133	_____	33	83	133	
34	84	134	_____	34	84	134	
35	85	135	_____	35	85	135	
36	86	136	_____	36	86	136	
37	87	137		37	87	137	
38	88	138	**NEW TESTAMENT**	38	88	138	
39	89	139		39	89	139	
40	90	140		40	90	140	
41	91	141	MATTHEW MARK LUKE JOHN ACTS ROMANS	41	91	141	
42	92	142	ICORINTHIANS IICORINTHIANS GALATIANS	42	92	142	
43	93	143	EPHESIANS PHILIPPIANS COLOSSIANS	43	93	143	
44	94	144	ITHESSALONIANS IITHESSALONIANS	44	94	144	
45	95	145		45	95	145	
46	96	146	ITIMOTHY IITIMOTHY TITUS PHILEMON	46	96	146	
47	97	147	HEBREWS JAMES IPETER IIPETER IJOHN	47	97	147	
48	98	148	IIJOHN IIIJOHN JUDE REVELATION	48	98	148	
49	99	149		49	99	149	
50	100	150		50	100	150	

NOTES

She is like the merchant's ships; she bringeth her food from afar.
-Proverbs 31:14 (KJV)

NOTES

She riseth also while ***it is*** yet night, and giveth meat to her
household, and a portion to her maidens.
-Proverbs 31:15 (KJV)

REFLECTIONS

_____
_____
_____
_____
_____
_____
_____
_____
_____
_____
_____
_____
_____
_____
_____
_____
_____
_____
_____
_____
_____
_____
_____
_____
_____
_____
_____
_____

She considereth a field, and buyeth it: with the fruit of her hands she planteth a vineyard.
-Proverbs 31:16 (KJV)

REFLECTIONS

She girdeth her lions with strength, and strengtheneth her arms.
-Proverbs 31:17 (KJV)

CHAPTER			OLD TESTAMENT	VERSE			

CHAPTER　　　　　**OLD TESTAMENT**　　　　　**VERSE**

1	51	101		1	51	101	151

GENESIS EXODUS LEVITICUS NUMBERS
DEUTERONOMY JOSHUA JUDGES RUTH ISAMUEL
IISAMUEL IKINGS IIKINGS ICHRONICLES
IICHRONICLES EZRA NEHEMIAH ESTHER JOB
PSALMS PROVERBS ECCLESIASTES SONG OF
SOLOMON ISAIAH JEREMIAH LAMENTATIONS
EZEKIEL DANIEL HOSEA JOEL AMOS
OBADIAH JONAH MICAH NAHUM HABAKKUK
ZEPHANIAH HAGGAI ZECHARIAH MALACHI

_____
_____
_____
_____
_____
_____
_____
_____
_____
_____
_____

NEW TESTAMENT

MATTHEW MARK LUKE JOHN ACTS ROMANS
ICORINTHIANS IICORINTHIANS GALATIANS
EPHESIANS PHILIPPIANS COLOSSIANS
ITHESSALONIANS IITHESSALONIANS
ITIMOTHY IITIMOTHY TITUS PHILEMON
HEBREWS JAMES IPETER IIPETER IJOHN
IIJOHN IIIJOHN JUDE REVELATION

_____
_____
_____
_____
_____
_____
_____
_____
_____

CHAPTER column:

1	51	101
2	52	102
3	53	103
4	54	104
5	55	105
6	56	106
7	57	107
8	58	108
9	59	109
10	60	110
11	61	111
12	62	112
13	63	113
14	64	114
15	65	115
16	66	116
17	67	117
18	68	118
19	69	119
20	70	120
21	71	121
22	72	122
23	73	123
24	74	124
25	75	125
26	76	126
27	77	127
28	78	128
29	79	129
30	80	130
31	81	131
32	82	132
33	83	133
34	84	134
35	85	135
36	86	136
37	87	137
38	88	138
39	89	139
40	90	140
41	91	141
42	92	142
43	93	143
44	94	144
45	95	145
46	96	146
47	97	147
48	98	148
49	99	149
50	100	150

VERSE column:

1	51	101	151
2	52	102	152
3	53	103	153
4	54	104	154
5	55	105	155
6	56	106	156
7	57	107	157
8	58	108	158
9	59	109	159
10	60	110	160
11	61	111	161
12	62	112	162
13	63	113	163
14	64	114	164
15	65	115	165
16	66	116	166
17	67	117	167
18	68	118	168
19	69	119	169
20	70	120	170
21	71	121	171
22	72	122	172
23	73	123	173
24	74	124	174
25	75	125	175
26	76	126	176
27	77	127	
28	78	128	
29	79	129	
30	80	130	
31	81	131	
32	82	132	
33	83	133	
34	84	134	
35	85	135	
36	86	136	
37	87	137	
38	88	138	
39	89	139	
40	90	140	
41	91	141	
42	92	142	
43	93	143	
44	94	144	
45	95	145	
46	96	146	
47	97	147	
48	98	148	
49	99	149	
50	100	150	

CHAPTER			OLD TESTAMENT	VERSE			
1	51	101	GENESIS EXODUS LEVITICUS NUMBERS	1	51	101	151
2	52	102	DEUTERONOMY JOSHUA JUDGES RUTH ISAMUEL	2	52	102	152
3	53	103		3	53	103	153
4	54	104	IISAMUEL IKINGS IIKINGS ICHRONICLES	4	54	104	154
5	55	105	IICHRONICLES EZRA NEHEMIAH ESTHER JOB	5	55	105	155
6	56	106		6	56	106	156
7	57	107	PSALMS PROVERBS ECCLESIASTES SONG OF	7	57	107	157
8	58	108	SOLOMON ISAIAH JEREMIAH LAMENTATIONS	8	58	108	158
9	59	109		9	59	109	159
10	60	110	EZEKIEL DANIEL HOSEA JOEL AMOS	10	60	110	160
11	61	111	OBADIAH JONAH MICAH NAHUM HABAKKUK	11	61	111	161
12	62	112		12	62	112	162
13	63	113	ZEPHANIAH HAGGAI ZECHARIAH MALACHI	13	63	113	163
14	64	114		14	64	114	164
15	65	115	_____	15	65	115	165
16	66	116	_____	16	66	116	166
17	67	117	_____	17	67	117	167
18	68	118	_____	18	68	118	168
19	69	119	_____	19	69	119	169
20	70	120	_____	20	70	120	170
21	71	121	_____	21	71	121	171
22	72	122	_____	22	72	122	172
23	73	123	_____	23	73	123	173
24	74	124	_____	24	74	124	174
25	75	125	_____	25	75	125	175
26	76	126	_____	26	76	126	176
27	77	127	_____	27	77	127	
28	78	128	_____	28	78	128	
29	79	129	_____	29	79	129	
30	80	130	_____	30	80	130	
31	81	131	_____	31	81	131	
32	82	132	_____	32	82	132	
33	83	133	_____	33	83	133	
34	84	134	_____	34	84	134	
35	85	135	_____	35	85	135	
36	86	136	_____	36	86	136	
37	87	137		37	87	137	
38	88	138		38	88	138	
39	89	139	**NEW TESTAMENT**	39	89	139	
40	90	140		40	90	140	
41	91	141	MATTHEW MARK LUKE JOHN ACTS ROMANS	41	91	141	
42	92	142	ICORINTHIANS IICORINTHIANS GALATIANS	42	92	142	
43	93	143		43	93	143	
44	94	144	EPHESIANS PHILIPPIANS COLOSSIANS	44	94	144	
45	95	145	ITHESSALONIANS IITHESSALONIANS	45	95	145	
46	96	146		46	96	146	
47	97	147	ITIMOTHY IITIMOTHY TITUS PHILEMON	47	97	147	
48	98	148	HEBREWS JAMES IPETER IIPETER IJOHN	48	98	148	
49	99	149	IIJOHN IIIJOHN JUDE REVELATION	49	99	149	
50	100	150		50	100	150	

NOTES

She perceiveth that her merchandise **is** good: her candle goeth not out by night.
**-Proverbs 31:18 (KJV)**

NOTES

She layeth her hands to the spindle, and her hands hold the distaff.
-Proverbs 31:19 (KJV)

REFLECTIONS

_____
_____
_____
_____
_____
_____
_____
_____
_____
_____
_____
_____
_____
_____
_____
_____
_____
_____
_____
_____
_____
_____
_____
_____
_____
_____
_____
_____
_____

She stretcheth out her hand to the poor; yea, she reacheth forth her hands to the needy.
-Proverbs 31:20 (KJV)

REFLECTIONS

*She is not afraid of the snow for her household: for all her household **are** clothed with scarlet.*
-Proverbs 31:21(KJV)

DATE _____

SPEAKER _____

TOPIC _____

CHAPTER

1	51	101
2	52	102
3	53	103
4	54	104
5	55	105
6	56	106
7	57	107
8	58	108
9	59	109
10	60	110
11	61	111
12	62	112
13	63	113
14	64	114
15	65	115
16	66	116
17	67	117
18	68	118
19	69	119
20	70	120
21	71	121
22	72	122
23	73	123
24	74	124
25	75	125
26	76	126
27	77	127
28	78	128
29	79	129
30	80	130
31	81	131
32	82	132
33	83	133
34	84	134
35	85	135
36	86	136
37	87	137
38	88	138
39	89	139
40	90	140
41	91	141
42	92	142
43	93	143
44	94	144
45	95	145
46	96	146
47	97	147
48	98	148
49	99	149
50	100	150

OLD TESTAMENT

GENESIS EXODUS LEVITICUS NUMBERS
DEUTERONOMY JOSHUA JUDGES RUTH ISAMUEL
IISAMUEL IKINGS IIKINGS ICHRONICLES
IICHRONICLES EZRA NEHEMIAH ESTHER JOB
PSALMS PROVERBS ECCLESIASTES SONG OF
SOLOMON ISAIAH JEREMIAH LAMENTATIONS
EZEKIEL DANIEL HOSEA JOEL AMOS
OBADIAH JONAH MICAH NAHUM HABAKKUK
ZEPHANIAH HAGGAI ZECHARIAH MALACHI

_____
_____
_____
_____
_____
_____
_____
_____
_____
_____
_____
_____

NEW TESTAMENT

MATTHEW MARK LUKE JOHN ACTS ROMANS
ICORINTHIANS IICORINTHIANS GALATIANS
EPHESIANS PHILIPPIANS COLOSSIANS
ITHESSALONIANS IITHESSALONIANS
ITIMOTHY IITIMOTHY TITUS PHILEMON
HEBREWS JAMES IPETER IIPETER IJOHN
IIJOHN IIIJOHN JUDE REVELATION

_____
_____
_____
_____
_____
_____
_____

VERSE

1	51	101	151
2	52	102	152
3	53	103	153
4	54	104	154
5	55	105	155
6	56	106	156
7	57	107	157
8	58	108	158
9	59	109	159
10	60	110	160
11	61	111	161
12	62	112	162
13	63	113	163
14	64	114	164
15	65	115	165
16	66	116	166
17	67	117	167
18	68	118	168
19	69	119	169
20	70	120	170
21	71	121	171
22	72	122	172
23	73	123	173
24	74	124	174
25	75	125	175
26	76	126	176
27	77	127	
28	78	128	
29	79	129	
30	80	130	
31	81	131	
32	82	132	
33	83	133	
34	84	134	
35	85	135	
36	86	136	
37	87	137	
38	88	138	
39	89	139	
40	90	140	
41	91	141	
42	92	142	
43	93	143	
44	94	144	
45	95	145	
46	96	146	
47	97	147	
48	98	148	
49	99	149	
50	100	150	

CHAPTER			OLD TESTAMENT	VERSE			

CHAPTER — OLD TESTAMENT — VERSE

GENESIS EXODUS LEVITICUS NUMBERS
DEUTERONOMY JOSHUA JUDGES RUTH ISAMUEL
IISAMUEL IKINGS IIKINGS ICHRONICLES
IICHRONICLES EZRA NEHEMIAH ESTHER JOB
PSALMS PROVERBS ECCLESIASTES SONG OF
SOLOMON ISAIAH JEREMIAH LAMENTATIONS
EZEKIEL DANIEL HOSEA JOEL AMOS
OBADIAH JONAH MICAH NAHUM HABAKKUK
ZEPHANIAH HAGGAI ZECHARIAH MALACHI

CHAPTER			VERSE			
1	51	101	1	51	101	151
2	52	102	2	52	102	152
3	53	103	3	53	103	153
4	54	104	4	54	104	154
5	55	105	5	55	105	155
6	56	106	6	56	106	156
7	57	107	7	57	107	157
8	58	108	8	58	108	158
9	59	109	9	59	109	159
10	60	110	10	60	110	160
11	61	111	11	61	111	161
12	62	112	12	62	112	162
13	63	113	13	63	113	163
14	64	114	14	64	114	164
15	65	115	15	65	115	165
16	66	116	16	66	116	166
17	67	117	17	67	117	167
18	68	118	18	68	118	168
19	69	119	19	69	119	169
20	70	120	20	70	120	170
21	71	121	21	71	121	171
22	72	122	22	72	122	172
23	73	123	23	73	123	173
24	74	124	24	74	124	174
25	75	125	25	75	125	175
26	76	126	26	76	126	176
27	77	127	27	77	127	
28	78	128	28	78	128	
29	79	129	29	79	129	
30	80	130	30	80	130	
31	81	131	31	81	131	
32	82	132	32	82	132	
33	83	133	33	83	133	
34	84	134	34	84	134	
35	85	135	35	85	135	
36	86	136	36	86	136	
37	87	137	37	87	137	
38	88	138	38	88	138	
39	89	139	39	89	139	
40	90	140	40	90	140	
41	91	141	41	91	141	
42	92	142	42	92	142	
43	93	143	43	93	143	
44	94	144	44	94	144	
45	95	145	45	95	145	
46	96	146	46	96	146	
47	97	147	47	97	147	
48	98	148	48	98	148	
49	99	149	49	99	149	
50	100	150	50	100	150	

NEW TESTAMENT

MATTHEW MARK LUKE JOHN ACTS ROMANS
ICORINTHIANS IICORINTHIANS GALATIANS
EPHESIANS PHILIPPIANS COLOSSIANS
ITHESSALONIANS IITHESSALONIANS
ITIMOTHY IITIMOTHY TITUS PHILEMON
HEBREWS JAMES IPETER IIPETER IJOHN
IIJOHN IIIJOHN JUDE REVELATION

NOTES

She maketh herself coverings of tapestry; her clothing **is** silk and purple.
-Proverbs 31:22 (KJV)

NOTES

_____

_____

_____

_____

_____

_____

_____

_____

_____

_____

_____

_____

_____

_____

_____

_____

_____

_____

_____

_____

_____

_____

_____

_____

_____

_____

_____

_____

Her husband is known in the gates, when he sitteth among the elders of the land.
-Proverbs 31:23 (KJV)

REFLECTIONS

She maketh fine linen, and selleth **it**; and delivereth girdles unto the merchant.
-Proverbs 31:24 (KJV)

REFLECTIONS

_____
_____
_____
_____
_____
_____
_____
_____
_____
_____
_____
_____
_____
_____
_____
_____
_____
_____
_____
_____
_____
_____
_____
_____
_____
_____
_____
_____
_____
_____
_____
_____
_____
_____

*Strength and honour **are** her clothing; and she shall rejoice in time to come.*
-Proverbs 31:25 (KJV)

DATE _____

SPEAKER _____

TOPIC _____

CHAPTER	OLD TESTAMENT	VERSE

CHAPTER

1	51	101
2	52	102
3	53	103
4	54	104
5	55	105
6	56	106
7	57	107
8	58	108
9	59	109
10	60	110
11	61	111
12	62	112
13	63	113
14	64	114
15	65	115
16	66	116
17	67	117
18	68	118
19	69	119
20	70	120
21	71	121
22	72	122
23	73	123
24	74	124
25	75	125
26	76	126
27	77	127
28	78	128
29	79	129
30	80	130
31	81	131
32	82	132
33	83	133
34	84	134
35	85	135
36	86	136
37	87	137
38	88	138
39	89	139
40	90	140
41	91	141
42	92	142
43	93	143
44	94	144
45	95	145
46	96	146
47	97	147
48	98	148
49	99	149
50	100	150

OLD TESTAMENT

GENESIS EXODUS LEVITICUS NUMBERS
DEUTERONOMY JOSHUA JUDGES RUTH ISAMUEL
IISAMUEL IKINGS IIKINGS ICHRONICLES
IICHRONICLES EZRA NEHEMIAH ESTHER JOB
PSALMS PROVERBS ECCLESIASTES SONG OF
SOLOMON ISAIAH JEREMIAH LAMENTATIONS
EZEKIEL DANIEL HOSEA JOEL AMOS
OBADIAH JONAH MICAH NAHUM HABAKKUK
ZEPHANIAH HAGGAI ZECHARIAH MALACHI

_____
_____
_____
_____
_____
_____
_____
_____
_____
_____
_____
_____

NEW TESTAMENT

MATTHEW MARK LUKE JOHN ACTS ROMANS
ICORINTHIANS IICORINTHIANS GALATIANS
EPHESIANS PHILIPPIANS COLOSSIANS
ITHESSALONIANS IITHESSALONIANS
ITIMOTHY IITIMOTHY TITUS PHILEMON
HEBREWS JAMES IPETER IIPETER IJOHN
IIJOHN IIIJOHN JUDE REVELATION

_____
_____
_____
_____
_____
_____
_____
_____

VERSE

1	51	101	151
2	52	102	152
3	53	103	153
4	54	104	154
5	55	105	155
6	56	106	156
7	57	107	157
8	58	108	158
9	59	109	159
10	60	110	160
11	61	111	161
12	62	112	162
13	63	113	163
14	64	114	164
15	65	115	165
16	66	116	166
17	67	117	167
18	68	118	168
19	69	119	169
20	70	120	170
21	71	121	171
22	72	122	172
23	73	123	173
24	74	124	174
25	75	125	175
26	76	126	176
27	77	127	
28	78	128	
29	79	129	
30	80	130	
31	81	131	
32	82	132	
33	83	133	
34	84	134	
35	85	135	
36	86	136	
37	87	137	
38	88	138	
39	89	139	
40	90	140	
41	91	141	
42	92	142	
43	93	143	
44	94	144	
45	95	145	
46	96	146	
47	97	147	
48	98	148	
49	99	149	
50	100	150	

CHAPTER			OLD TESTAMENT	VERSE			
1	51	101	GENESIS EXODUS LEVITICUS NUMBERS	1	51	101	151
2	52	102	DEUTERONOMY JOSHUA JUDGES RUTH ISAMUEL	2	52	102	152
3	53	103	IISAMUEL IKINGS IIKINGS ICHRONICLES	3	53	103	153
4	54	104	IICHRONICLES EZRA NEHEMIAH ESTHER JOB	4	54	104	154
5	55	105	PSALMS PROVERBS ECCLESIASTES SONG OF	5	55	105	155
6	56	106	SOLOMON ISAIAH JEREMIAH LAMENTATIONS	6	56	106	156
7	57	107	EZEKIEL DANIEL HOSEA JOEL AMOS	7	57	107	157
8	58	108	OBADIAH JONAH MICAH NAHUM HABAKKUK	8	58	108	158
9	59	109	ZEPHANIAH HAGGAI ZECHARIAH MALACHI	9	59	109	159
10	60	110		10	60	110	160
11	61	111		11	61	111	161
12	62	112		12	62	112	162
13	63	113		13	63	113	163
14	64	114	_____	14	64	114	164
15	65	115	_____	15	65	115	165
16	66	116	_____	16	66	116	166
17	67	117	_____	17	67	117	167
18	68	118	_____	18	68	118	168
19	69	119	_____	19	69	119	169
20	70	120	_____	20	70	120	170
21	71	121	_____	21	71	121	171
22	72	122	_____	22	72	122	172
23	73	123	_____	23	73	123	173
24	74	124	_____	24	74	124	174
25	75	125	_____	25	75	125	175
26	76	126	_____	26	76	126	176
27	77	127	_____	27	77	127	
28	78	128	_____	28	78	128	
29	79	129	_____	29	79	129	
30	80	130	_____	30	80	130	
31	81	131	_____	31	81	131	
32	82	132	_____	32	82	132	
33	83	133	_____	33	83	133	
34	84	134	_____	34	84	134	
35	85	135	_____	35	85	135	
36	86	136	_____	36	86	136	
37	87	137		37	87	137	
38	88	138	**NEW TESTAMENT**	38	88	138	
39	89	139		39	89	139	
40	90	140		40	90	140	
41	91	141	MATTHEW MARK LUKE JOHN ACTS ROMANS	41	91	141	
42	92	142	ICORINTHIANS IICORINTHIANS GALATIANS	42	92	142	
43	93	143	EPHESIANS PHILIPPIANS COLOSSIANS	43	93	143	
44	94	144	ITHESSALONIANS IITHESSALONIANS	44	94	144	
45	95	145	ITIMOTHY IITIMOTHY TITUS PHILEMON	45	95	145	
46	96	146	HEBREWS JAMES IPETER IIPETER IJOHN	46	96	146	
47	97	147	IIJOHN IIIJOHN JUDE REVELATION	47	97	147	
48	98	148		48	98	148	
49	99	149		49	99	149	
50	100	150		50	100	150	

NOTES

She openeth her mouth with wisdom; and in her tongue **is** the law of kindness.
-Proverbs 31:26 (KJV)

NOTES

She looketh well to the ways of her household, and eateth not the bread of idleness.
-Proverbs 31:27 (KJV)

REFLECTIONS

Her children arise up, and call her blessed; her husband **also**, and he praiseth her.
-Proverbs 31:28 (KJV)

REFLECTIONS

_____
_____
_____
_____
_____
_____
_____
_____
_____
_____
_____
_____
_____
_____
_____
_____
_____
_____
_____
_____
_____
_____
_____
_____
_____
_____
_____
_____
_____
_____
_____

Many daughters have done virtuously, but thou excellest them all.
-Proverbs 31:29 (KJV)

CHAPTER

1	51	101
2	52	102
3	53	103
4	54	104
5	55	105
6	56	106
7	57	107
8	58	108
9	59	109
10	60	110
11	61	111
12	62	112
13	63	113
14	64	114
15	65	115
16	66	116
17	67	117
18	68	118
19	69	119
20	70	120
21	71	121
22	72	122
23	73	123
24	74	124
25	75	125
26	76	126
27	77	127
28	78	128
29	79	129
30	80	130
31	81	131
32	82	132
33	83	133
34	84	134
35	85	135
36	86	136
37	87	137
38	88	138
39	89	139
40	90	140
41	91	141
42	92	142
43	93	143
44	94	144
45	95	145
46	96	146
47	97	147
48	98	148
49	99	149
50	100	150

OLD TESTAMENT

GENESIS EXODUS LEVITICUS NUMBERS
DEUTERONOMY JOSHUA JUDGES RUTH ISAMUEL
IISAMUEL IKINGS IIKINGS ICHRONICLES
IICHRONICLES EZRA NEHEMIAH ESTHER JOB
PSALMS PROVERBS ECCLESIASTES SONG OF
SOLOMON ISAIAH JEREMIAH LAMENTATIONS
EZEKIEL DANIEL HOSEA JOEL AMOS
OBADIAH JONAH MICAH NAHUM HABAKKUK
ZEPHANIAH HAGGAI ZECHARIAH MALACHI

_____
_____
_____
_____
_____
_____
_____
_____
_____
_____
_____
_____

NEW TESTAMENT

MATTHEW MARK LUKE JOHN ACTS ROMANS
ICORINTHIANS IICORINTHIANS GALATIANS
EPHESIANS PHILIPPIANS COLOSSIANS
ITHESSALONIANS IITHESSALONIANS
ITIMOTHY IITIMOTHY TITUS PHILEMON
HEBREWS JAMES IPETER IIPETER IJOHN
IIJOHN IIIJOHN JUDE REVELATION

_____
_____
_____
_____
_____
_____
_____
_____

VERSE

1	51	101	151
2	52	102	152
3	53	103	153
4	54	104	154
5	55	105	155
6	56	106	156
7	57	107	157
8	58	108	158
9	59	109	159
10	60	110	160
11	61	111	161
12	62	112	162
13	63	113	163
14	64	114	164
15	65	115	165
16	66	116	166
17	67	117	167
18	68	118	168
19	69	119	169
20	70	120	170
21	71	121	171
22	72	122	172
23	73	123	173
24	74	124	174
25	75	125	175
26	76	126	176
27	77	127	
28	78	128	
29	79	129	
30	80	130	
31	81	131	
32	82	132	
33	83	133	
34	84	134	
35	85	135	
36	86	136	
37	87	137	
38	88	138	
39	89	139	
40	90	140	
41	91	141	
42	92	142	
43	93	143	
44	94	144	
45	95	145	
46	96	146	
47	97	147	
48	98	148	
49	99	149	
50	100	150	

CHAPTER			OLD TESTAMENT	VERSE			
1	51	101		1	51	101	151
2	52	102	GENESIS EXODUS LEVITICUS NUMBERS	2	52	102	152
3	53	103	DEUTERONOMY JOSHUA JUDGES RUTH ISAMUEL	3	53	103	153
4	54	104	IISAMUEL IKINGS IIKINGS ICHRONICLES	4	54	104	154
5	55	105	IICHRONICLES EZRA NEHEMIAH ESTHER JOB	5	55	105	155
6	56	106	PSALMS PROVERBS ECCLESIASTES SONG OF	6	56	106	156
7	57	107	SOLOMON ISAIAH JEREMIAH LAMENTATIONS	7	57	107	157
8	58	108	EZEKIEL DANIEL HOSEA JOEL AMOS	8	58	108	158
9	59	109	OBADIAH JONAH MICAH NAHUM HABAKKUK	9	59	109	159
10	60	110	ZEPHANIAH HAGGAI ZECHARIAH MALACHI	10	60	110	160
11	61	111		11	61	111	161
12	62	112		12	62	112	162
13	63	113	_____	13	63	113	163
14	64	114	_____	14	64	114	164
15	65	115	_____	15	65	115	165
16	66	116	_____	16	66	116	166
17	67	117	_____	17	67	117	167
18	68	118	_____	18	68	118	168
19	69	119	_____	19	69	119	169
20	70	120	_____	20	70	120	170
21	71	121	_____	21	71	121	171
22	72	122	_____	22	72	122	172
23	73	123	_____	23	73	123	173
24	74	124	_____	24	74	124	174
25	75	125	_____	25	75	125	175
26	76	126	_____	26	76	126	176
27	77	127	_____	27	77	127	
28	78	128	_____	28	78	128	
29	79	129	_____	29	79	129	
30	80	130	_____	30	80	130	
31	81	131	_____	31	81	131	
32	82	132	_____	32	82	132	
33	83	133	_____	33	83	133	
34	84	134	_____	34	84	134	
35	85	135	_____	35	85	135	
36	86	136	_____	36	86	136	
37	87	137		37	87	137	
38	88	138		38	88	138	
39	89	139	**NEW TESTAMENT**	39	89	139	
40	90	140		40	90	140	
41	91	141	MATTHEW MARK LUKE JOHN ACTS ROMANS	41	91	141	
42	92	142	ICORINTHIANS IICORINTHIANS GALATIANS	42	92	142	
43	93	143	EPHESIANS PHILIPPIANS COLOSSIANS	43	93	143	
44	94	144	ITHESSALONIANS IITHESSALONIANS	44	94	144	
45	95	145	ITIMOTHY IITIMOTHY TITUS PHILEMON	45	95	145	
46	96	146	HEBREWS JAMES IPETER IIPETER IJOHN	46	96	146	
47	97	147	IIJOHN IIIJOHN JUDE REVELATION	47	97	147	
48	98	148		48	98	148	
49	99	149		49	99	149	
50	100	150		50	100	150	

NOTES

Favour **is** deceitful, and beauty **is** vain; **but** a woman **that**
feareth the **LORD**, she shall be praised.
**-Proverbs 31:30 (KJV)**

NOTES

_____

_____

_____

_____

_____

_____

_____

_____

_____

_____

_____

_____

_____

_____

_____

_____

_____

_____

_____

_____

_____

_____

_____

_____

_____

_____

_____

_____

_____

Give her of the fruit of her hands; and let her own works praise her in the gates.
-Proverbs 31:31 (KJV)

REFLECTIONS

_____
_____
_____
_____
_____
_____
_____
_____
_____
_____
_____
_____
_____
_____
_____
_____
_____
_____
_____
_____
_____
_____
_____
_____
_____
_____
_____

A wife of noble character who can find? She is worth far more than rubies.
–Proverbs 31: 10(NIV)

REFLECTIONS

Her husband has full confidence in her and lacks nothing of value.
-Proverbs 31: 11(NIV)

CHAPTER

1	51	101
2	52	102
3	53	103
4	54	104
5	55	105
6	56	106
7	57	107
8	58	108
9	59	109
10	60	110
11	61	111
12	62	112
13	63	113
14	64	114
15	65	115
16	66	116
17	67	117
18	68	118
19	69	119
20	70	120
21	71	121
22	72	122
23	73	123
24	74	124
25	75	125
26	76	126
27	77	127
28	78	128
29	79	129
30	80	130
31	81	131
32	82	132
33	83	133
34	84	134
35	85	135
36	86	136
37	87	137
38	88	138
39	89	139
40	90	140
41	91	141
42	92	142
43	93	143
44	94	144
45	95	145
46	96	146
47	97	147
48	98	148
49	99	149
50	100	150

OLD TESTAMENT

GENESIS EXODUS LEVITICUS NUMBERS
DEUTERONOMY JOSHUA JUDGES RUTH ISAMUEL
IISAMUEL IKINGS IIKINGS ICHRONICLES
IICHRONICLES EZRA NEHEMIAH ESTHER JOB
PSALMS PROVERBS ECCLESIASTES SONG OF
SOLOMON ISAIAH JEREMIAH LAMENTATIONS
EZEKIEL DANIEL HOSEA JOEL AMOS
OBADIAH JONAH MICAH NAHUM HABAKKUK
ZEPHANIAH HAGGAI ZECHARIAH MALACHI

_____

_____

_____

_____

_____

_____

_____

_____

_____

_____

_____

_____

NEW TESTAMENT

MATTHEW MARK LUKE JOHN ACTS ROMANS
ICORINTHIANS IICORINTHIANS GALATIANS
EPHESIANS PHILIPPIANS COLOSSIANS
ITHESSALONIANS IITHESSALONIANS
ITIMOTHY IITIMOTHY TITUS PHILEMON
HEBREWS JAMES IPETER IIPETER IJOHN
IIJOHN IIIJOHN JUDE REVELATION

_____

_____

_____

_____

_____

_____

_____

VERSE

1	51	101	151
2	52	102	152
3	53	103	153
4	54	104	154
5	55	105	155
6	56	106	156
7	57	107	157
8	58	108	158
9	59	109	159
10	60	110	160
11	61	111	161
12	62	112	162
13	63	113	163
14	64	114	164
15	65	115	165
16	66	116	166
17	67	117	167
18	68	118	168
19	69	119	169
20	70	120	170
21	71	121	171
22	72	122	172
23	73	123	173
24	74	124	174
25	75	125	175
26	76	126	176
27	77	127	
28	78	128	
29	79	129	
30	80	130	
31	81	131	
32	82	132	
33	83	133	
34	84	134	
35	85	135	
36	86	136	
37	87	137	
38	88	138	
39	89	139	
40	90	140	
41	91	141	
42	92	142	
43	93	143	
44	94	144	
45	95	145	
46	96	146	
47	97	147	
48	98	148	
49	99	149	
50	100	150	

CHAPTER			OLD TESTAMENT	VERSE			
1	51	101		1	51	101	151
2	52	102	GENESIS EXODUS LEVITICUS NUMBERS	2	52	102	152
3	53	103	DEUTERONOMY JOSHUA JUDGES RUTH ISAMUEL	3	53	103	153
4	54	104	IISAMUEL IKINGS IIKINGS ICHRONICLES	4	54	104	154
5	55	105	IICHRONICLES EZRA NEHEMIAH ESTHER JOB	5	55	105	155
6	56	106	IICHRONICLES EZRA NEHEMIAH ESTHER JOB	6	56	106	156
7	57	107	PSALMS PROVERBS ECCLESIASTES SONG OF	7	57	107	157
8	58	108	SOLOMON ISAIAH JEREMIAH LAMENTATIONS	8	58	108	158
9	59	109	SOLOMON ISAIAH JEREMIAH LAMENTATIONS	9	59	109	159
10	60	110	EZEKIEL DANIEL HOSEA JOEL AMOS	10	60	110	160
11	61	111	EZEKIEL DANIEL HOSEA JOEL AMOS	11	61	111	161
12	62	112	OBADIAH JONAH MICAH NAHUM HABAKKUK	12	62	112	162
13	63	113	ZEPHANIAH HAGGAI ZECHARIAH MALACHI	13	63	113	163
14	64	114		14	64	114	164
15	65	115	_____	15	65	115	165
16	66	116	_____	16	66	116	166
17	67	117	_____	17	67	117	167
18	68	118	_____	18	68	118	168
19	69	119	_____	19	69	119	169
20	70	120	_____	20	70	120	170
21	71	121	_____	21	71	121	171
22	72	122	_____	22	72	122	172
23	73	123	_____	23	73	123	173
24	74	124	_____	24	74	124	174
25	75	125	_____	25	75	125	175
26	76	126	_____	26	76	126	176
27	77	127	_____	27	77	127	
28	78	128	_____	28	78	128	
29	79	129	_____	29	79	129	
30	80	130	_____	30	80	130	
31	81	131	_____	31	81	131	
32	82	132	_____	32	82	132	
33	83	133	_____	33	83	133	
34	84	134	_____	34	84	134	
35	85	135	_____	35	85	135	
36	86	136	_____	36	86	136	
37	87	137		37	87	137	
38	88	138		38	88	138	
39	89	139	NEW TESTAMENT	39	89	139	
40	90	140		40	90	140	
41	91	141	MATTHEW MARK LUKE JOHN ACTS ROMANS	41	91	141	
42	92	142	ICORINTHIANS IICORINTHIANS GALATIANS	42	92	142	
43	93	143	ICORINTHIANS IICORINTHIANS GALATIANS	43	93	143	
44	94	144	EPHESIANS PHILIPPIANS COLOSSIANS	44	94	144	
45	95	145	ITHESSALONIANS IITHESSALONIANS	45	95	145	
46	96	146	ITHESSALONIANS IITHESSALONIANS	46	96	146	
47	97	147	ITIMOTHY IITIMOTHY TITUS PHILEMON	47	97	147	
48	98	148	HEBREWS JAMES IPETER IIPETER IJOHN	48	98	148	
49	99	149	HEBREWS JAMES IPETER IIPETER IJOHN	49	99	149	
50	100	150	IIJOHN IIIJOHN JUDE REVELATION	50	100	150	

NOTES

She brings him good, not harm, all the days of her life.
-Proverbs 31: 12 (NIV)

NOTES

_____
_____
_____
_____
_____
_____
_____
_____
_____
_____
_____
_____
_____
_____
_____
_____
_____
_____
_____
_____
_____
_____
_____
_____
_____
_____
_____
_____

She selects wool and flax and works with eager hands.
-Proverbs 31: 13(NIV)

REFLECTIONS

_____
_____
_____
_____
_____
_____
_____
_____
_____
_____
_____
_____
_____
_____
_____
_____
_____
_____
_____
_____
_____
_____
_____
_____
_____
_____
_____
_____

She is like the merchant ships, bringing her food from afar.
-Proverbs 31:14(NIV)

REFLECTIONS

_____

_____

_____

_____

_____

_____

_____

_____

_____

_____

_____

_____

_____

_____

_____

_____

_____

_____

_____

_____

_____

_____

_____

_____

_____

_____

_____

_____

_____

_____

_____

She gets up while it is still dark; she provides food for her
family and portions for her servant girls.
-Proverbs 31:15(NIV)

CHAPTER			OLD TESTAMENT	VERSE			
1	51	101	GENESIS EXODUS LEVITICUS NUMBERS	1	51	101	151
2	52	102		2	52	102	152
3	53	103	DEUTERONOMY JOSHUA JUDGES RUTH ISAMUEL	3	53	103	153
4	54	104	IISAMUEL IKINGS IIKINGS ICHRONICLES	4	54	104	154
5	55	105		5	55	105	155
6	56	106	IICHRONICLES EZRA NEHEMIAH ESTHER JOB	6	56	106	156
7	57	107	PSALMS PROVERBS ECCLESIASTES SONG OF	7	57	107	157
8	58	108		8	58	108	158
9	59	109	SOLOMON ISAIAH JEREMIAH LAMENTATIONS	9	59	109	159
10	60	110	EZEKIEL DANIEL HOSEA JOEL AMOS	10	60	110	160
11	61	111		11	61	111	161
12	62	112	OBADIAH JONAH MICAH NAHUM HABAKKUK	12	62	112	162
13	63	113	ZEPHANIAH HAGGAI ZECHARIAH MALACHI	13	63	113	163
14	64	114		14	64	114	164
15	65	115	_____	15	65	115	165
16	66	116	_____	16	66	116	166
17	67	117	_____	17	67	117	167
18	68	118	_____	18	68	118	168
19	69	119	_____	19	69	119	169
20	70	120	_____	20	70	120	170
21	71	121	_____	21	71	121	171
22	72	122	_____	22	72	122	172
23	73	123	_____	23	73	123	173
24	74	124	_____	24	74	124	174
25	75	125	_____	25	75	125	175
26	76	126	_____	26	76	126	176
27	77	127	_____	27	77	127	
28	78	128		28	78	128	
29	79	129	NEW TESTAMENT	29	79	129	
30	80	130		30	80	130	
31	81	131	MATTHEW MARK LUKE JOHN ACTS ROMANS	31	81	131	
32	82	132	ICORINTHIANS IICORINTHIANS GALATIANS	32	82	132	
33	83	133		33	83	133	
34	84	134	EPHESIANS PHILIPPIANS COLOSSIANS	34	84	134	
35	85	135	ITHESSALONIANS IITHESSALONIANS	35	85	135	
36	86	136		36	86	136	
37	87	137	ITIMOTHY IITIMOTHY TITUS PHILEMON	37	87	137	
38	88	138	HEBREWS JAMES IPETER IIPETER IJOHN	38	88	138	
39	89	139		39	89	139	
40	90	140	IIJOHN IIIJOHN JUDE REVELATION	40	90	140	
41	91	141	_____	41	91	141	
42	92	142	_____	42	92	142	
43	93	143	_____	43	93	143	
44	94	144	_____	44	94	144	
45	95	145	_____	45	95	145	
46	96	146	_____	46	96	146	
47	97	147	_____	47	97	147	
48	98	148	_____	48	98	148	
49	99	149	_____	49	99	149	
50	100	150	_____	50	100	150	

CHAPTER			OLD TESTAMENT	VERSE			
1	51	101		1	51	101	151
2	52	102	GENESIS EXODUS LEVITICUS NUMBERS	2	52	102	152
3	53	103	DEUTERONOMY JOSHUA JUDGES RUTH ISAMUEL	3	53	103	153
4	54	104	IISAMUEL IKINGS IIKINGS ICHRONICLES	4	54	104	154
5	55	105	IICHRONICLES EZRA NEHEMIAH ESTHER JOB	5	55	105	155
6	56	106	PSALMS PROVERBS ECCLESIASTES SONG OF	6	56	106	156
7	57	107	SOLOMON ISAIAH JEREMIAH LAMENTATIONS	7	57	107	157
8	58	108	EZEKIEL DANIEL HOSEA JOEL AMOS	8	58	108	158
9	59	109	OBADIAH JONAH MICAH NAHUM HABAKKUK	9	59	109	159
10	60	110	ZEPHANIAH HAGGAI ZECHARIAH MALACHI	10	60	110	160
11	61	111		11	61	111	161
12	62	112		12	62	112	162
13	63	113	_____	13	63	113	163
14	64	114	_____	14	64	114	164
15	65	115	_____	15	65	115	165
16	66	116	_____	16	66	116	166
17	67	117	_____	17	67	117	167
18	68	118	_____	18	68	118	168
19	69	119	_____	19	69	119	169
20	70	120	_____	20	70	120	170
21	71	121	_____	21	71	121	171
22	72	122	_____	22	72	122	172
23	73	123	_____	23	73	123	173
24	74	124	_____	24	74	124	174
25	75	125	_____	25	75	125	175
26	76	126	_____	26	76	126	176
27	77	127	_____	27	77	127	
28	78	128	_____	28	78	128	
29	79	129	_____	29	79	129	
30	80	130	_____	30	80	130	
31	81	131	_____	31	81	131	
32	82	132	_____	32	82	132	
33	83	133	_____	33	83	133	
34	84	134	_____	34	84	134	
35	85	135	_____	35	85	135	
36	86	136	_____	36	86	136	
37	87	137		37	87	137	
38	88	138		38	88	138	
39	89	139	NEW TESTAMENT	39	89	139	
40	90	140		40	90	140	
41	91	141	MATTHEW MARK LUKE JOHN ACTS ROMANS	41	91	141	
42	92	142	ICORINTHIANS IICORINTHIANS GALATIANS	42	92	142	
43	93	143	EPHESIANS PHILIPPIANS COLOSSIANS	43	93	143	
44	94	144	ITHESSALONIANS IITHESSALONIANS	44	94	144	
45	95	145	ITIMOTHY IITIMOTHY TITUS PHILEMON	45	95	145	
46	96	146	HEBREWS JAMES IPETER IIPETER IJOHN	46	96	146	
47	97	147	IIJOHN IIIJOHN JUDE REVELATION	47	97	147	
48	98	148		48	98	148	
49	99	149		49	99	149	
50	100	150		50	100	150	

NOTES

She considers a field and buys it; out of her earnings she plants a vineyard.
-Proverbs 31:16(NIV)

NOTES

She sets about her work vigorously; her arms are strong for her tasks.
-Proverbs 31:17(NIV)

REFLECTIONS

She sees that her trading is profitable, and her lamp does not go out at night.
-Proverbs 31:18(NIV)

REFLECTIONS

In her hand she holds the distaff and grasps the spindle with her fingers.
-Proverbs 31:19(NIV)

DATE _____

SPEAKER _____

TOPIC _____

CHAPTER			OLD TESTAMENT	VERSE			

CHAPTER

1   51   101
2   52   102
3   53   103
4   54   104
5   55   105
6   56   106
7   57   107
8   58   108
9   59   109
10   60   110
11   61   111
12   62   112
13   63   113
14   64   114
15   65   115
16   66   116
17   67   117
18   68   118
19   69   119
20   70   120
21   71   121
22   72   122
23   73   123
24   74   124
25   75   125
26   76   126
27   77   127
28   78   128
29   79   129
30   80   130
31   81   131
32   82   132
33   83   133
34   84   134
35   85   135
36   86   136
37   87   137
38   88   138
39   89   139
40   90   140
41   91   141
42   92   142
43   93   143
44   94   144
45   95   145
46   96   146
47   97   147
48   98   148
49   99   149
50   100   150

OLD TESTAMENT

GENESIS EXODUS LEVITICUS NUMBERS
DEUTERONOMY JOSHUA JUDGES RUTH ISAMUEL
IISAMUEL IKINGS IIKINGS ICHRONICLES
IICHRONICLES EZRA NEHEMIAH ESTHER JOB
PSALMS PROVERBS ECCLESIASTES SONG OF
SOLOMON ISAIAH JEREMIAH LAMENTATIONS
EZEKIEL DANIEL HOSEA JOEL AMOS
OBADIAH JONAH MICAH NAHUM HABAKKUK
ZEPHANIAH HAGGAI ZECHARIAH MALACHI

_____
_____
_____
_____
_____
_____
_____
_____
_____
_____
_____
_____

NEW TESTAMENT

MATTHEW MARK LUKE JOHN ACTS ROMANS
ICORINTHIANS IICORINTHIANS GALATIANS
EPHESIANS PHILIPPIANS COLOSSIANS
ITHESSALONIANS IITHESSALONIANS
ITIMOTHY IITIMOTHY TITUS PHILEMON
HEBREWS JAMES IPETER IIPETER IJOHN
IIJOHN IIIJOHN JUDE REVELATION

_____
_____
_____
_____
_____
_____
_____

VERSE

1   51   101   151
2   52   102   152
3   53   103   153
4   54   104   154
5   55   105   155
6   56   106   156
7   57   107   157
8   58   108   158
9   59   109   159
10   60   110   160
11   61   111   161
12   62   112   162
13   63   113   163
14   64   114   164
15   65   115   165
16   66   116   166
17   67   117   167
18   68   118   168
19   69   119   169
20   70   120   170
21   71   121   171
22   72   122   172
23   73   123   173
24   74   124   174
25   75   125   175
26   76   126   176
27   77   127
28   78   128
29   79   129
30   80   130
31   81   131
32   82   132
33   83   133
34   84   134
35   85   135
36   86   136
37   87   137
38   88   138
39   89   139
40   90   140
41   91   141
42   92   142
43   93   143
44   94   144
45   95   145
46   96   146
47   97   147
48   98   148
49   99   149
50   100   150

CHAPTER			OLD TESTAMENT	VERSE			
1	51	101		1	51	101	151
2	52	102	GENESIS EXODUS LEVITICUS NUMBERS	2	52	102	152
3	53	103	DEUTERONOMY JOSHUA JUDGES RUTH ISAMUEL	3	53	103	153
4	54	104	IISAMUEL IKINGS IIKINGS ICHRONICLES	4	54	104	154
5	55	105		5	55	105	155
6	56	106	IICHRONICLES EZRA NEHEMIAH ESTHER JOB	6	56	106	156
7	57	107	PSALMS PROVERBS ECCLESIASTES SONG OF	7	57	107	157
8	58	108	SOLOMON ISAIAH JEREMIAH LAMENTATIONS	8	58	108	158
9	59	109		9	59	109	159
10	60	110	EZEKIEL DANIEL HOSEA JOEL AMOS	10	60	110	160
11	61	111	OBADIAH JONAH MICAH NAHUM HABAKKUK	11	61	111	161
12	62	112	ZEPHANIAH HAGGAI ZECHARIAH MALACHI	12	62	112	162
13	63	113		13	63	113	163
14	64	114	_____	14	64	114	164
15	65	115	_____	15	65	115	165
16	66	116	_____	16	66	116	166
17	67	117	_____	17	67	117	167
18	68	118	_____	18	68	118	168
19	69	119	_____	19	69	119	169
20	70	120	_____	20	70	120	170
21	71	121	_____	21	71	121	171
22	72	122	_____	22	72	122	172
23	73	123	_____	23	73	123	173
24	74	124	_____	24	74	124	174
25	75	125	_____	25	75	125	175
26	76	126	_____	26	76	126	176
27	77	127	_____	27	77	127	
28	78	128	_____	28	78	128	
29	79	129	_____	29	79	129	
30	80	130	_____	30	80	130	
31	81	131	_____	31	81	131	
32	82	132	_____	32	82	132	
33	83	133	_____	33	83	133	
34	84	134	_____	34	84	134	
35	85	135	_____	35	85	135	
36	86	136	_____	36	86	136	
37	87	137		37	87	137	
38	88	138		38	88	138	
39	89	139	NEW TESTAMENT	39	89	139	
40	90	140		40	90	140	
41	91	141	MATTHEW MARK LUKE JOHN ACTS ROMANS	41	91	141	
42	92	142	ICORINTHIANS IICORINTHIANS GALATIANS	42	92	142	
43	93	143	EPHESIANS PHILIPPIANS COLOSSIANS	43	93	143	
44	94	144	ITHESSALONIANS IITHESSALONIANS	44	94	144	
45	95	145		45	95	145	
46	96	146	ITIMOTHY IITIMOTHY TITUS PHILEMON	46	96	146	
47	97	147	HEBREWS JAMES IPETER IIPETER IJOHN	47	97	147	
48	98	148	IIJOHN IIIJOHN JUDE REVELATION	48	98	148	
49	99	149		49	99	149	
50	100	150		50	100	150	

NOTES

She opens her arms to the poor and extends her hands to the needy.
-Proverbs 31:20(NIV)

NOTES

When it snows, she has not fear for her household; for all of them are clothed in scarlet.
-Proverbs 31:21(NIV)

REFLECTIONS

She makes coverings for her bed; she is clothed in fine linen and purple.
-Proverbs 31:22(NIV)

REFLECTIONS

_____
_____
_____
_____
_____
_____
_____
_____
_____
_____
_____
_____
_____
_____
_____
_____
_____
_____
_____
_____
_____
_____
_____
_____
_____
_____
_____
_____

When it snows, she has not fear for her household for all of them are clothed in scarlet.
-Proverbs 31:21(NIV)

CHAPTER	OLD TESTAMENT	VERSE

CHAPTER

1	51	101
2	52	102
3	53	103
4	54	104
5	55	105
6	56	106
7	57	107
8	58	108
9	59	109
10	60	110
11	61	111
12	62	112
13	63	113
14	64	114
15	65	115
16	66	116
17	67	117
18	68	118
19	69	119
20	70	120
21	71	121
22	72	122
23	73	123
24	74	124
25	75	125
26	76	126
27	77	127
28	78	128
29	79	129
30	80	130
31	81	131
32	82	132
33	83	133
34	84	134
35	85	135
36	86	136
37	87	137
38	88	138
39	89	139
40	90	140
41	91	141
42	92	142
43	93	143
44	94	144
45	95	145
46	96	146
47	97	147
48	98	148
49	99	149
50	100	150

OLD TESTAMENT

GENESIS EXODUS LEVITICUS NUMBERS
DEUTERONOMY JOSHUA JUDGES RUTH ISAMUEL
IISAMUEL IKINGS IIKINGS ICHRONICLES
IICHRONICLES EZRA NEHEMIAH ESTHER JOB
PSALMS PROVERBS ECCLESIASTES SONG OF
SOLOMON ISAIAH JEREMIAH LAMENTATIONS
EZEKIEL DANIEL HOSEA JOEL AMOS
OBADIAH JONAH MICAH NAHUM HABAKKUK
ZEPHANIAH HAGGAI ZECHARIAH MALACHI

_____
_____
_____
_____
_____
_____
_____
_____
_____
_____
_____
_____

NEW TESTAMENT

MATTHEW MARK LUKE JOHN ACTS ROMANS
ICORINTHIANS IICORINTHIANS GALATIANS
EPHESIANS PHILIPPIANS COLOSSIANS
ITHESSALONIANS IITHESSALONIANS
ITIMOTHY IITIMOTHY TITUS PHILEMON
HEBREWS JAMES IPETER IIPETER IJOHN
IIJOHN IIIJOHN JUDE REVELATION

_____
_____
_____
_____
_____
_____
_____

VERSE

1	51	101	151
2	52	102	152
3	53	103	153
4	54	104	154
5	55	105	155
6	56	106	156
7	57	107	157
8	58	108	158
9	59	109	159
10	60	110	160
11	61	111	161
12	62	112	162
13	63	113	163
14	64	114	164
15	65	115	165
16	66	116	166
17	67	117	167
18	68	118	168
19	69	119	169
20	70	120	170
21	71	121	171
22	72	122	172
23	73	123	173
24	74	124	174
25	75	125	175
26	76	126	176
27	77	127	
28	78	128	
29	79	129	
30	80	130	
31	81	131	
32	82	132	
33	83	133	
34	84	134	
35	85	135	
36	86	136	
37	87	137	
38	88	138	
39	89	139	
40	90	140	
41	91	141	
42	92	142	
43	93	143	
44	94	144	
45	95	145	
46	96	146	
47	97	147	
48	98	148	
49	99	149	
50	100	150	

CHAPTER

1	51	101
2	52	102
3	53	103
4	54	104
5	55	105
6	56	106
7	57	107
8	58	108
9	59	109
10	60	110
11	61	111
12	62	112
13	63	113
14	64	114
15	65	115
16	66	116
17	67	117
18	68	118
19	69	119
20	70	120
21	71	121
22	72	122
23	73	123
24	74	124
25	75	125
26	76	126
27	77	127
28	78	128
29	79	129
30	80	130
31	81	131
32	82	132
33	83	133
34	84	134
35	85	135
36	86	136
37	87	137
38	88	138
39	89	139
40	90	140
41	91	141
42	92	142
43	93	143
44	94	144
45	95	145
46	96	146
47	97	147
48	98	148
49	99	149
50	100	150

OLD TESTAMENT

GENESIS EXODUS LEVITICUS NUMBERS
DEUTERONOMY JOSHUA JUDGES RUTH ISAMUEL
IISAMUEL IKINGS IIKINGS ICHRONICLES
IICHRONICLES EZRA NEHEMIAH ESTHER JOB
PSALMS PROVERBS ECCLESIASTES SONG OF
SOLOMON ISAIAH JEREMIAH LAMENTATIONS
EZEKIEL DANIEL HOSEA JOEL AMOS
OBADIAH JONAH MICAH NAHUM HABAKKUK
ZEPHANIAH HAGGAI ZECHARIAH MALACHI

_____
_____
_____
_____
_____
_____
_____
_____
_____
_____
_____
_____
_____
_____
_____
_____
_____
_____
_____
_____
_____

NEW TESTAMENT

MATTHEW MARK LUKE JOHN ACTS ROMANS
ICORINTHIANS IICORINTHIANS GALATIANS
EPHESIANS PHILIPPIANS COLOSSIANS
ITHESSALONIANS IITHESSALONIANS
ITIMOTHY IITIMOTHY TITUS PHILEMON
HEBREWS JAMES IPETER IIPETER IJOHN
IIJOHN IIIJOHN JUDE REVELATION

VERSE

1	51	101	151
2	52	102	152
3	53	103	153
4	54	104	154
5	55	105	155
6	56	106	156
7	57	107	157
8	58	108	158
9	59	109	159
10	60	110	160
11	61	111	161
12	62	112	162
13	63	113	163
14	64	114	164
15	65	115	165
16	66	116	166
17	67	117	167
18	68	118	168
19	69	119	169
20	70	120	170
21	71	121	171
22	72	122	172
23	73	123	173
24	74	124	174
25	75	125	175
26	76	126	176
27	77	127	
28	78	128	
29	79	129	
30	80	130	
31	81	131	
32	82	132	
33	83	133	
34	84	134	
35	85	135	
36	86	136	
37	87	137	
38	88	138	
39	89	139	
40	90	140	
41	91	141	
42	92	142	
43	93	143	
44	94	144	
45	95	145	
46	96	146	
47	97	147	
48	98	148	
49	99	149	
50	100	150	

NOTES

Her husband is respected at the city gate, where he takes his seat among the elders of the land.
-Proverbs 31:23(NIV)

NOTES

She makes linen garments and sells them, and supplies the merchants with sashes.
-Proverbs 31:24(NIV)

REFLECTIONS

She is clothed with strength and dignity; she can laugh at the days to come.
-Proverbs 31:25 (NIV)

REFLECTIONS

_____
_____
_____
_____
_____
_____
_____
_____
_____
_____
_____
_____
_____
_____
_____
_____
_____
_____
_____
_____
_____
_____
_____
_____
_____
_____
_____
_____
_____
_____

She speaks with wisdom, and faithful instruction is on her tongue.
-Proverbs 31:26(NIV)

CHAPTER			OLD TESTAMENT	VERSE			

CHAPTER

1	51	101
2	52	102
3	53	103
4	54	104
5	55	105
6	56	106
7	57	107
8	58	108
9	59	109
10	60	110
11	61	111
12	62	112
13	63	113
14	64	114
15	65	115
16	66	116
17	67	117
18	68	118
19	69	119
20	70	120
21	71	121
22	72	122
23	73	123
24	74	124
25	75	125
26	76	126
27	77	127
28	78	128
29	79	129
30	80	130
31	81	131
32	82	132
33	83	133
34	84	134
35	85	135
36	86	136
37	87	137
38	88	138
39	89	139
40	90	140
41	91	141
42	92	142
43	93	143
44	94	144
45	95	145
46	96	146
47	97	147
48	98	148
49	99	149
50	100	150

OLD TESTAMENT

GENESIS EXODUS LEVITICUS NUMBERS
DEUTERONOMY JOSHUA JUDGES RUTH ISAMUEL
IISAMUEL IKINGS IIKINGS ICHRONICLES
IICHRONICLES EZRA NEHEMIAH ESTHER JOB
PSALMS PROVERBS ECCLESIASTES SONG OF
SOLOMON ISAIAH JEREMIAH LAMENTATIONS
EZEKIEL DANIEL HOSEA JOEL AMOS
OBADIAH JONAH MICAH NAHUM HABAKKUK
ZEPHANIAH HAGGAI ZECHARIAH MALACHI

_____
_____
_____
_____
_____
_____
_____
_____
_____
_____
_____
_____

NEW TESTAMENT

MATTHEW MARK LUKE JOHN ACTS ROMANS
ICORINTHIANS IICORINTHIANS GALATIANS
EPHESIANS PHILIPPIANS COLOSSIANS
ITHESSALONIANS IITHESSALONIANS
ITIMOTHY IITIMOTHY TITUS PHILEMON
HEBREWS JAMES IPETER IIPETER IJOHN
IIJOHN IIIJOHN JUDE REVELATION

_____
_____
_____
_____
_____
_____
_____
_____

VERSE

1	51	101	151
2	52	102	152
3	53	103	153
4	54	104	154
5	55	105	155
6	56	106	156
7	57	107	157
8	58	108	158
9	59	109	159
10	60	110	160
11	61	111	161
12	62	112	162
13	63	113	163
14	64	114	164
15	65	115	165
16	66	116	166
17	67	117	167
18	68	118	168
19	69	119	169
20	70	120	170
21	71	121	171
22	72	122	172
23	73	123	173
24	74	124	174
25	75	125	175
26	76	126	176
27	77	127	
28	78	128	
29	79	129	
30	80	130	
31	81	131	
32	82	132	
33	83	133	
34	84	134	
35	85	135	
36	86	136	
37	87	137	
38	88	138	
39	89	139	
40	90	140	
41	91	141	
42	92	142	
43	93	143	
44	94	144	
45	95	145	
46	96	146	
47	97	147	
48	98	148	
49	99	149	
50	100	150	

CHAPTER			OLD TESTAMENT	VERSE			
1	51	101		1	51	101	151
2	52	102	GENESIS EXODUS LEVITICUS NUMBERS	2	52	102	152
3	53	103	DEUTERONOMY JOSHUA JUDGES RUTH ISAMUEL	3	53	103	153
4	54	104	IISAMUEL IKINGS IIKINGS ICHRONICLES	4	54	104	154
5	55	105	IISAMUEL IKINGS IIKINGS ICHRONICLES	5	55	105	155
6	56	106	IICHRONICLES EZRA NEHEMIAH ESTHER JOB	6	56	106	156
7	57	107	PSALMS PROVERBS ECCLESIASTES SONG OF	7	57	107	157
8	58	108	SOLOMON ISAIAH JEREMIAH LAMENTATIONS	8	58	108	158
9	59	109	SOLOMON ISAIAH JEREMIAH LAMENTATIONS	9	59	109	159
10	60	110	EZEKIEL DANIEL HOSEA JOEL AMOS	10	60	110	160
11	61	111	OBADIAH JONAH MICAH NAHUM HABAKKUK	11	61	111	161
12	62	112	OBADIAH JONAH MICAH NAHUM HABAKKUK	12	62	112	162
13	63	113	ZEPHANIAH HAGGAI ZECHARIAH MALACHI	13	63	113	163
14	64	114		14	64	114	164
15	65	115	_____	15	65	115	165
16	66	116	_____	16	66	116	166
17	67	117	_____	17	67	117	167
18	68	118	_____	18	68	118	168
19	69	119	_____	19	69	119	169
20	70	120	_____	20	70	120	170
21	71	121	_____	21	71	121	171
22	72	122	_____	22	72	122	172
23	73	123	_____	23	73	123	173
24	74	124	_____	24	74	124	174
25	75	125	_____	25	75	125	175
26	76	126	_____	26	76	126	176
27	77	127	_____	27	77	127	
28	78	128	_____	28	78	128	
29	79	129	_____	29	79	129	
30	80	130	_____	30	80	130	
31	81	131	_____	31	81	131	
32	82	132	_____	32	82	132	
33	83	133	_____	33	83	133	
34	84	134	_____	34	84	134	
35	85	135	_____	35	85	135	
36	86	136	_____	36	86	136	
37	87	137		37	87	137	
38	88	138	NEW TESTAMENT	38	88	138	
39	89	139		39	89	139	
40	90	140		40	90	140	
41	91	141	MATTHEW MARK LUKE JOHN ACTS ROMANS	41	91	141	
42	92	142	ICORINTHIANS IICORINTHIANS GALATIANS	42	92	142	
43	93	143	ICORINTHIANS IICORINTHIANS GALATIANS	43	93	143	
44	94	144	EPHESIANS PHILIPPIANS COLOSSIANS	44	94	144	
45	95	145	ITHESSALONIANS IITHESSALONIANS	45	95	145	
46	96	146	ITHESSALONIANS IITHESSALONIANS	46	96	146	
47	97	147	ITIMOTHY IITIMOTHY TITUS PHILEMON	47	97	147	
48	98	148	HEBREWS JAMES IPETER IIPETER IJOHN	48	98	148	
49	99	149	HEBREWS JAMES IPETER IIPETER IJOHN	49	99	149	
50	100	150	IIJOHN IIIJOHN JUDE REVELATION	50	100	150	

NOTES

She watches over the affairs of her household and does not eat the bread of idleness.
-Proverbs 31:27(NIV)

NOTES

_____
_____
_____
_____
_____
_____
_____
_____
_____
_____
_____
_____
_____
_____
_____
_____
_____
_____
_____
_____
_____
_____
_____
_____
_____
_____
_____
_____
_____
_____
_____

Her children arise and call her blessed; her husband also, and he praises her:
-Proverbs 31:28(NIV)

REFLECTIONS

"Many women do noble things, but you surpass them all."
-Proverbs 31:29 (NIV)

REFLECTIONS

_____
_____
_____
_____
_____
_____
_____
_____
_____
_____
_____
_____
_____
_____
_____
_____
_____
_____
_____
_____
_____
_____
_____
_____
_____
_____
_____
_____
_____

Charm is deceptive, and beauty is fleeting; but a woman who fears the LORD is to be praise.
-Proverbs 31:30(NIV)

CHAPTER			OLD TESTAMENT	VERSE			

CHAPTER / OLD TESTAMENT / VERSE

CHAPTER			VERSE			
1	51	101	1	51	101	151
2	52	102	2	52	102	152
3	53	103	3	53	103	153
4	54	104	4	54	104	154
5	55	105	5	55	105	155
6	56	106	6	56	106	156
7	57	107	7	57	107	157
8	58	108	8	58	108	158
9	59	109	9	59	109	159
10	60	110	10	60	110	160
11	61	111	11	61	111	161
12	62	112	12	62	112	162
13	63	113	13	63	113	163
14	64	114	14	64	114	164
15	65	115	15	65	115	165
16	66	116	16	66	116	166
17	67	117	17	67	117	167
18	68	118	18	68	118	168
19	69	119	19	69	119	169
20	70	120	20	70	120	170
21	71	121	21	71	121	171
22	72	122	22	72	122	172
23	73	123	23	73	123	173
24	74	124	24	74	124	174
25	75	125	25	75	125	175
26	76	126	26	76	126	176
27	77	127	27	77	127	
28	78	128	28	78	128	
29	79	129	29	79	129	
30	80	130	30	80	130	
31	81	131	31	81	131	
32	82	132	32	82	132	
33	83	133	33	83	133	
34	84	134	34	84	134	
35	85	135	35	85	135	
36	86	136	36	86	136	
37	87	137	37	87	137	
38	88	138	38	88	138	
39	89	139	39	89	139	
40	90	140	40	90	140	
41	91	141	41	91	141	
42	92	142	42	92	142	
43	93	143	43	93	143	
44	94	144	44	94	144	
45	95	145	45	95	145	
46	96	146	46	96	146	
47	97	147	47	97	147	
48	98	148	48	98	148	
49	99	149	49	99	149	
50	100	150	50	100	150	

OLD TESTAMENT

GENESIS EXODUS LEVITICUS NUMBERS
DEUTERONOMY JOSHUA JUDGES RUTH ISAMUEL
IISAMUEL IKINGS IIKINGS ICHRONICLES
IICHRONICLES EZRA NEHEMIAH ESTHER JOB
PSALMS PROVERBS ECCLESIASTES SONG OF
SOLOMON ISAIAH JEREMIAH LAMENTATIONS
EZEKIEL DANIEL HOSEA JOEL AMOS
OBADIAH JONAH MICAH NAHUM HABAKKUK
ZEPHANIAH HAGGAI ZECHARIAH MALACHI

_____

_____

_____

_____

_____

_____

_____

_____

_____

_____

_____

_____

NEW TESTAMENT

MATTHEW MARK LUKE JOHN ACTS ROMANS
ICORINTHIANS IICORINTHIANS GALATIANS
EPHESIANS PHILIPPIANS COLOSSIANS
ITHESSALONIANS IITHESSALONIANS
ITIMOTHY IITIMOTHY TITUS PHILEMON
HEBREWS JAMES IPETER IIPETER IJOHN
IIJOHN IIIJOHN JUDE REVELATION

_____

_____

_____

_____

_____

_____

_____

_____

CHAPTER			OLD TESTAMENT	VERSE			
1	51	101	GENESIS EXODUS LEVITICUS NUMBERS	1	51	101	151
2	52	102	DEUTERONOMY JOSHUA JUDGES RUTH ISAMUEL	2	52	102	152
3	53	103	IISAMUEL IKINGS IIKINGS ICHRONICLES	3	53	103	153
4	54	104	IICHRONICLES EZRA NEHEMIAH ESTHER JOB	4	54	104	154
5	55	105	PSALMS PROVERBS ECCLESIASTES SONG OF	5	55	105	155
6	56	106	SOLOMON ISAIAH JEREMIAH LAMENTATIONS	6	56	106	156
7	57	107	EZEKIEL DANIEL HOSEA JOEL AMOS	7	57	107	157
8	58	108	OBADIAH JONAH MICAH NAHUM HABAKKUK	8	58	108	158
9	59	109	ZEPHANIAH HAGGAI ZECHARIAH MALACHI	9	59	109	159
10	60	110		10	60	110	160
11	61	111		11	61	111	161
12	62	112		12	62	112	162
13	63	113		13	63	113	163
14	64	114	_____	14	64	114	164
15	65	115	_____	15	65	115	165
16	66	116	_____	16	66	116	166
17	67	117	_____	17	67	117	167
18	68	118	_____	18	68	118	168
19	69	119	_____	19	69	119	169
20	70	120	_____	20	70	120	170
21	71	121	_____	21	71	121	171
22	72	122	_____	22	72	122	172
23	73	123	_____	23	73	123	173
24	74	124	_____	24	74	124	174
25	75	125	_____	25	75	125	175
26	76	126	_____	26	76	126	176
27	77	127	_____	27	77	127	
28	78	128	_____	28	78	128	
29	79	129	_____	29	79	129	
30	80	130	_____	30	80	130	
31	81	131	_____	31	81	131	
32	82	132	_____	32	82	132	
33	83	133	_____	33	83	133	
34	84	134	_____	34	84	134	
35	85	135	_____	35	85	135	
36	86	136	_____	36	86	136	
37	87	137		37	87	137	
38	88	138	**NEW TESTAMENT**	38	88	138	
39	89	139		39	89	139	
40	90	140		40	90	140	
41	91	141	MATTHEW MARK LUKE JOHN ACTS ROMANS	41	91	141	
42	92	142	ICORINTHIANS IICORINTHIANS GALATIANS	42	92	142	
43	93	143	EPHESIANS PHILIPPIANS COLOSSIANS	43	93	143	
44	94	144	ITHESSALONIANS IITHESSALONIANS	44	94	144	
45	95	145	ITIMOTHY IITIMOTHY TITUS PHILEMON	45	95	145	
46	96	146	HEBREWS JAMES IPETER IIPETER IJOHN	46	96	146	
47	97	147	IIJOHN IIIJOHN JUDE REVELATION	47	97	147	
48	98	148		48	98	148	
49	99	149		49	99	149	
50	100	150		50	100	150	

NOTES

Give her the reward she has earned, and let her works bring her praise at the city gate.
-Proverbs 31:31(NIV)

NOTES

_____

_____

_____

_____

_____

_____

_____

_____

_____

_____

_____

_____

_____

_____

_____

_____

_____

_____

_____

_____

_____

_____

_____

_____

_____

_____

_____

_____

_____

Who can find a virtuous and capable wife? She is worth more than precious rubies.
-Proverbs 31:10 (NLTV)

REFLECTIONS

_____
_____
_____
_____
_____
_____
_____
_____
_____
_____
_____
_____
_____
_____
_____
_____
_____
_____
_____
_____
_____
_____
_____
_____
_____
_____
_____
_____
_____

Her husband can trust her, and she will greatly enrich his life.
-Proverbs 31:11(NLT)

REFLECTIONS

She will not hinder him but held him all her life.
-Proverbs 31:12(NLT)

DATE _____
SPEAKER _____
TOPIC _____

CHAPTER			OLD TESTAMENT	VERSE			
1	51	101	GENESIS EXODUS LEVITICUS NUMBERS	1	51	101	151
2	52	102	DEUTERONOMY JOSHUA JUDGES RUTH ISAMUEL	2	52	102	152
3	53	103	IISAMUEL IKINGS IIKINGS ICHRONICLES	3	53	103	153
4	54	104	IICHRONICLES EZRA NEHEMIAH ESTHER JOB	4	54	104	154
5	55	105	PSALMS PROVERBS ECCLESIASTES SONG OF	5	55	105	155
6	56	106	SOLOMON ISAIAH JEREMIAH LAMENTATIONS	6	56	106	156
7	57	107	EZEKIEL DANIEL HOSEA JOEL AMOS	7	57	107	157
8	58	108	OBADIAH JONAH MICAH NAHUM HABAKKUK	8	58	108	158
9	59	109	ZEPHANIAH HAGGAI ZECHARIAH MALACHI	9	59	109	159
10	60	110		10	60	110	160
11	61	111		11	61	111	161
12	62	112		12	62	112	162
13	63	113		13	63	113	163
14	64	114	_____	14	64	114	164
15	65	115	_____	15	65	115	165
16	66	116	_____	16	66	116	166
17	67	117	_____	17	67	117	167
18	68	118	_____	18	68	118	168
19	69	119	_____	19	69	119	169
20	70	120	_____	20	70	120	170
21	71	121	_____	21	71	121	171
22	72	122	_____	22	72	122	172
23	73	123	_____	23	73	123	173
24	74	124	_____	24	74	124	174
25	75	125	_____	25	75	125	175
26	76	126	_____	26	76	126	176
27	77	127		27	77	127	
28	78	128		28	78	128	
29	79	129	NEW TESTAMENT	29	79	129	
30	80	130		30	80	130	
31	81	131	MATTHEW MARK LUKE JOHN ACTS ROMANS	31	81	131	
32	82	132	ICORINTHIANS IICORINTHIANS GALATIANS	32	82	132	
33	83	133	EPHESIANS PHILIPPIANS COLOSSIANS	33	83	133	
34	84	134	ITHESSALONIANS IITHESSALONIANS	34	84	134	
35	85	135	ITIMOTHY IITIMOTHY TITUS PHILEMON	35	85	135	
36	86	136	HEBREWS JAMES IPETER IIPETER IJOHN	36	86	136	
37	87	137	IIJOHN IIIJOHN JUDE REVELATION	37	87	137	
38	88	138		38	88	138	
39	89	139		39	89	139	
40	90	140		40	90	140	
41	91	141	_____	41	91	141	
42	92	142	_____	42	92	142	
43	93	143	_____	43	93	143	
44	94	144	_____	44	94	144	
45	95	145	_____	45	95	145	
46	96	146	_____	46	96	146	
47	97	147	_____	47	97	147	
48	98	148	_____	48	98	148	
49	99	149	_____	49	99	149	
50	100	150	_____	50	100	150	

CHAPTER			OLD TESTAMENT	VERSE			

CHAPTER

1	51	101
2	52	102
3	53	103
4	54	104
5	55	105
6	56	106
7	57	107
8	58	108
9	59	109
10	60	110
11	61	111
12	62	112
13	63	113
14	64	114
15	65	115
16	66	116
17	67	117
18	68	118
19	69	119
20	70	120
21	71	121
22	72	122
23	73	123
24	74	124
25	75	125
26	76	126
27	77	127
28	78	128
29	79	129
30	80	130
31	81	131
32	82	132
33	83	133
34	84	134
35	85	135
36	86	136
37	87	137
38	88	138
39	89	139
40	90	140
41	91	141
42	92	142
43	93	143
44	94	144
45	95	145
46	96	146
47	97	147
48	98	148
49	99	149
50	100	150

OLD TESTAMENT

GENESIS EXODUS LEVITICUS NUMBERS
DEUTERONOMY JOSHUA JUDGES RUTH ISAMUEL
IISAMUEL IKINGS IIKINGS ICHRONICLES
IICHRONICLES EZRA NEHEMIAH ESTHER JOB
PSALMS PROVERBS ECCLESIASTES SONG OF
SOLOMON ISAIAH JEREMIAH LAMENTATIONS
EZEKIEL DANIEL HOSEA JOEL AMOS
OBADIAH JONAH MICAH NAHUM HABAKKUK
ZEPHANIAH HAGGAI ZECHARIAH MALACHI

NEW TESTAMENT

MATTHEW MARK LUKE JOHN ACTS ROMANS
ICORINTHIANS IICORINTHIANS GALATIANS
EPHESIANS PHILIPPIANS COLOSSIANS
ITHESSALONIANS IITHESSALONIANS
ITIMOTHY IITIMOTHY TITUS PHILEMON
HEBREWS JAMES IPETER IIPETER IJOHN
IIJOHN IIIJOHN JUDE REVELATION

VERSE

1	51	101	151
2	52	102	152
3	53	103	153
4	54	104	154
5	55	105	155
6	56	106	156
7	57	107	157
8	58	108	158
9	59	109	159
10	60	110	160
11	61	111	161
12	62	112	162
13	63	113	163
14	64	114	164
15	65	115	165
16	66	116	166
17	67	117	167
18	68	118	168
19	69	119	169
20	70	120	170
21	71	121	171
22	72	122	172
23	73	123	173
24	74	124	174
25	75	125	175
26	76	126	176
27	77	127	
28	78	128	
29	79	129	
30	80	130	
31	81	131	
32	82	132	
33	83	133	
34	84	134	
35	85	135	
36	86	136	
37	87	137	
38	88	138	
39	89	139	
40	90	140	
41	91	141	
42	92	142	
43	93	143	
44	94	144	
45	95	145	
46	96	146	
47	97	147	
48	98	148	
49	99	149	
50	100	150	

NOTES

She finds wool and flax and busily spins it.
-Proverbs 31:13(NLT)

NOTES

She is like a merchant's ship; she brings her food from afar.
-Proverbs 31:14(NLT)

REFLECTIONS

_____

_____

_____

_____

_____

_____

_____

_____

_____

_____

_____

_____

_____

_____

_____

_____

_____

_____

_____

_____

_____

_____

_____

_____

_____

_____

_____

_____

_____

She gets up before dawn to prepare breakfast for her household
and plan the day's work for her servant girls.
-Proverbs 31:15(NLT)

REFLECTIONS

_____
_____
_____
_____
_____
_____
_____
_____
_____
_____
_____
_____
_____
_____
_____
_____
_____
_____
_____
_____
_____
_____
_____
_____
_____
_____
_____
_____
_____
_____

She goes out to inspect a field and buys it; with her earnings she plants vineyard.
-Proverbs 31:16(NLT)

CHAPTER			OLD TESTAMENT	VERSE			
1	51	101		1	51	101	151
2	52	102	GENESIS EXODUS LEVITICUS NUMBERS	2	52	102	152
3	53	103	DEUTERONOMY JOSHUA JUDGES RUTH ISAMUEL	3	53	103	153
4	54	104	IISAMUEL IKINGS IIKINGS ICHRONICLES	4	54	104	154
5	55	105	IICHRONICLES EZRA NEHEMIAH ESTHER JOB	5	55	105	155
6	56	106	PSALMS PROVERBS ECCLESIASTES SONG OF	6	56	106	156
7	57	107	SOLOMON ISAIAH JEREMIAH LAMENTATIONS	7	57	107	157
8	58	108	EZEKIEL DANIEL HOSEA JOEL AMOS	8	58	108	158
9	59	109	OBADIAH JONAH MICAH NAHUM HABAKKUK	9	59	109	159
10	60	110	ZEPHANIAH HAGGAI ZECHARIAH MALACHI	10	60	110	160
11	61	111		11	61	111	161
12	62	112		12	62	112	162
13	63	113		13	63	113	163
14	64	114		14	64	114	164
15	65	115	_____	15	65	115	165
16	66	116	_____	16	66	116	166
17	67	117	_____	17	67	117	167
18	68	118	_____	18	68	118	168
19	69	119	_____	19	69	119	169
20	70	120	_____	20	70	120	170
21	71	121	_____	21	71	121	171
22	72	122	_____	22	72	122	172
23	73	123	_____	23	73	123	173
24	74	124	_____	24	74	124	174
25	75	125	_____	25	75	125	175
26	76	126	_____	26	76	126	176
27	77	127	_____	27	77	127	
28	78	128		28	78	128	
29	79	129	NEW TESTAMENT	29	79	129	
30	80	130		30	80	130	
31	81	131	MATTHEW MARK LUKE JOHN ACTS ROMANS	31	81	131	
32	82	132	ICORINTHIANS IICORINTHIANS GALATIANS	32	82	132	
33	83	133	EPHESIANS PHILIPPIANS COLOSSIANS	33	83	133	
34	84	134	ITHESSALONIANS IITHESSALONIANS	34	84	134	
35	85	135	ITIMOTHY IITIMOTHY TITUS PHILEMON	35	85	135	
36	86	136	HEBREWS JAMES IPETER IIPETER IJOHN	36	86	136	
37	87	137	IIJOHN IIIJOHN JUDE REVELATION	37	87	137	
38	88	138		38	88	138	
39	89	139		39	89	139	
40	90	140		40	90	140	
41	91	141	_____	41	91	141	
42	92	142	_____	42	92	142	
43	93	143	_____	43	93	143	
44	94	144	_____	44	94	144	
45	95	145	_____	45	95	145	
46	96	146	_____	46	96	146	
47	97	147	_____	47	97	147	
48	98	148	_____	48	98	148	
49	99	149	_____	49	99	149	
50	100	150	_____	50	100	150	

CHAPTER

1	51	101
2	52	102
3	53	103
4	54	104
5	55	105
6	56	106
7	57	107
8	58	108
9	59	109
10	60	110
11	61	111
12	62	112
13	63	113
14	64	114
15	65	115
16	66	116
17	67	117
18	68	118
19	69	119
20	70	120
21	71	121
22	72	122
23	73	123
24	74	124
25	75	125
26	76	126
27	77	127
28	78	128
29	79	129
30	80	130
31	81	131
32	82	132
33	83	133
34	84	134
35	85	135
36	86	136
37	87	137
38	88	138
39	89	139
40	90	140
41	91	141
42	92	142
43	93	143
44	94	144
45	95	145
46	96	146
47	97	147
48	98	148
49	99	149
50	100	150

OLD TESTAMENT

GENESIS EXODUS LEVITICUS NUMBERS
DEUTERONOMY JOSHUA JUDGES RUTH ISAMUEL
IISAMUEL IKINGS IIKINGS ICHRONICLES
IICHRONICLES EZRA NEHEMIAH ESTHER JOB
PSALMS PROVERBS ECCLESIASTES SONG OF
SOLOMON ISAIAH JEREMIAH LAMENTATIONS
EZEKIEL DANIEL HOSEA JOEL AMOS
OBADIAH JONAH MICAH NAHUM HABAKKUK
ZEPHANIAH HAGGAI ZECHARIAH MALACHI

_____

_____

_____

_____

_____

_____

_____

_____

_____

_____

_____

_____

_____

_____

_____

_____

_____

_____

_____

NEW TESTAMENT

MATTHEW MARK LUKE JOHN ACTS ROMANS
ICORINTHIANS IICORINTHIANS GALATIANS
EPHESIANS PHILIPPIANS COLOSSIANS
ITHESSALONIANS IITHESSALONIANS
ITIMOTHY IITIMOTHY TITUS PHILEMON
HEBREWS JAMES IPETER IIPETER IJOHN
IIJOHN IIIJOHN JUDE REVELATION

VERSE

1	51	101	151
2	52	102	152
3	53	103	153
4	54	104	154
5	55	105	155
6	56	106	156
7	57	107	157
8	58	108	158
9	59	109	159
10	60	110	160
11	61	111	161
12	62	112	162
13	63	113	163
14	64	114	164
15	65	115	165
16	66	116	166
17	67	117	167
18	68	118	168
19	69	119	169
20	70	120	170
21	71	121	171
22	72	122	172
23	73	123	173
24	74	124	174
25	75	125	175
26	76	126	176
27	77	127	
28	78	128	
29	79	129	
30	80	130	
31	81	131	
32	82	132	
33	83	133	
34	84	134	
35	85	135	
36	86	136	
37	87	137	
38	88	138	
39	89	139	
40	90	140	
41	91	141	
42	92	142	
43	93	143	
44	94	144	
45	95	145	
46	96	146	
47	97	147	
48	98	148	
49	99	149	
50	100	150	

NOTES

She is energetic and strong, a hard worker.
-Proverbs 31:17(NLT)

NOTES

She watches for bargains; her lights burn late into the night.
-Proverbs 31:18(NLT)

REFLECTIONS

_____
_____
_____
_____
_____
_____
_____
_____
_____
_____
_____
_____
_____
_____
_____
_____
_____
_____
_____
_____
_____
_____
_____
_____
_____
_____
_____
_____

Her hands are busy spinning thread, her fingers twisting fiber.
-Proverbs 31:19 (NLT)

REFLECTIONS

She extends a helping hand to the poor and opens her arms to the needy.
-Proverbs 31:20(NLT)

CHAPTER | OLD TESTAMENT | VERSE

CHAPTER			OLD TESTAMENT	VERSE			
1	51	101	**GENESIS EXODUS LEVITICUS NUMBERS**	1	51	101	151
2	52	102	DEUTERONOMY JOSHUA JUDGES RUTH ISAMUEL	2	52	102	152
3	53	103	IISAMUEL IKINGS IIKINGS ICHRONICLES	3	53	103	153
4	54	104	IICHRONICLES EZRA NEHEMIAH ESTHER JOB	4	54	104	154
5	55	105	PSALMS PROVERBS ECCLESIASTES SONG OF	5	55	105	155
6	56	106	SOLOMON ISAIAH JEREMIAH LAMENTATIONS	6	56	106	156
7	57	107	EZEKIEL DANIEL HOSEA JOEL AMOS	7	57	107	157
8	58	108	OBADIAH JONAH MICAH NAHUM HABAKKUK	8	58	108	158
9	59	109	ZEPHANIAH HAGGAI ZECHARIAH MALACHI	9	59	109	159
10	60	110		10	60	110	160
11	61	111		11	61	111	161
12	62	112		12	62	112	162
13	63	113		13	63	113	163
14	64	114	_____	14	64	114	164
15	65	115	_____	15	65	115	165
16	66	116	_____	16	66	116	166
17	67	117	_____	17	67	117	167
18	68	118	_____	18	68	118	168
19	69	119	_____	19	69	119	169
20	70	120	_____	20	70	120	170
21	71	121	_____	21	71	121	171
22	72	122	_____	22	72	122	172
23	73	123	_____	23	73	123	173
24	74	124	_____	24	74	124	174
25	75	125	_____	25	75	125	175
26	76	126	_____	26	76	126	176
27	77	127		27	77	127	
28	78	128		28	78	128	
29	79	129	**NEW TESTAMENT**	29	79	129	
30	80	130		30	80	130	
31	81	131	MATTHEW MARK LUKE JOHN ACTS ROMANS	31	81	131	
32	82	132	ICORINTHIANS IICORINTHIANS GALATIANS	32	82	132	
33	83	133	EPHESIANS PHILIPPIANS COLOSSIANS	33	83	133	
34	84	134	ITHESSALONIANS IITHESSALONIANS	34	84	134	
35	85	135	ITIMOTHY IITIMOTHY TITUS PHILEMON	35	85	135	
36	86	136	HEBREWS JAMES IPETER IIPETER IJOHN	36	86	136	
37	87	137	IIJOHN IIIJOHN JUDE REVELATION	37	87	137	
38	88	138		38	88	138	
39	89	139		39	89	139	
40	90	140		40	90	140	
41	91	141		41	91	141	
42	92	142	_____	42	92	142	
43	93	143	_____	43	93	143	
44	94	144	_____	44	94	144	
45	95	145	_____	45	95	145	
46	96	146	_____	46	96	146	
47	97	147	_____	47	97	147	
48	98	148	_____	48	98	148	
49	99	149	_____	49	99	149	
50	100	150	_____	50	100	150	

CHAPTER

OLD TESTAMENT

VERSE

1	51	101
2	52	102
3	53	103
4	54	104
5	55	105
6	56	106
7	57	107
8	58	108
9	59	109
10	60	110
11	61	111
12	62	112
13	63	113
14	64	114
15	65	115
16	66	116
17	67	117
18	68	118
19	69	119
20	70	120
21	71	121
22	72	122
23	73	123
24	74	124
25	75	125
26	76	126
27	77	127
28	78	128
29	79	129
30	80	130
31	81	131
32	82	132
33	83	133
34	84	134
35	85	135
36	86	136
37	87	137
38	88	138
39	89	139
40	90	140
41	91	141
42	92	142
43	93	143
44	94	144
45	95	145
46	96	146
47	97	147
48	98	148
49	99	149
50	100	150

GENESIS EXODUS LEVITICUS NUMBERS
DEUTERONOMY JOSHUA JUDGES RUTH ISAMUEL
IISAMUEL IKINGS IIKINGS ICHRONICLES
IICHRONICLES EZRA NEHEMIAH ESTHER JOB
PSALMS PROVERBS ECCLESIASTES SONG OF
SOLOMON ISAIAH JEREMIAH LAMENTATIONS
EZEKIEL DANIEL HOSEA JOEL AMOS
OBADIAH JONAH MICAH NAHUM HABAKKUK
ZEPHANIAH HAGGAI ZECHARIAH MALACHI

_____
_____
_____
_____
_____
_____
_____
_____
_____
_____
_____
_____
_____
_____
_____
_____
_____
_____
_____
_____
_____
_____

NEW TESTAMENT

MATTHEW MARK LUKE JOHN ACTS ROMANS
ICORINTHIANS IICORINTHIANS GALATIANS
EPHESIANS PHILIPPIANS COLOSSIANS
ITHESSALONIANS IITHESSALONIANS
ITIMOTHY IITIMOTHY TITUS PHILEMON
HEBREWS JAMES IPETER IIPETER IJOHN
IIJOHN IIIJOHN JUDE REVELATION

1	51	101	151
2	52	102	152
3	53	103	153
4	54	104	154
5	55	105	155
6	56	106	156
7	57	107	157
8	58	108	158
9	59	109	159
10	60	110	160
11	61	111	161
12	62	112	162
13	63	113	163
14	64	114	164
15	65	115	165
16	66	116	166
17	67	117	167
18	68	118	168
19	69	119	169
20	70	120	170
21	71	121	171
22	72	122	172
23	73	123	173
24	74	124	174
25	75	125	175
26	76	126	176
27	77	127	
28	78	128	
29	79	129	
30	80	130	
31	81	131	
32	82	132	
33	83	133	
34	84	134	
35	85	135	
36	86	136	
37	87	137	
38	88	138	
39	89	139	
40	90	140	
41	91	141	
42	92	142	
43	93	143	
44	94	144	
45	95	145	
46	96	146	
47	97	147	
48	98	148	
49	99	149	
50	100	150	

NOTES

She has no fear of winter for her household because all of them have warm clothes.
-Proverbs 31:21(NLT)

NOTES

She quilts her own bedspreads. She dresses like royalty in gowns of finest cloth.
-Proverbs 31:22(NLT)

REFLECTIONS

Her husband is well known, for he sits in the council meeting with the other civic leaders.
-Proverbs 31:23(NLT)

REFLECTIONS

_____
_____
_____
_____
_____
_____
_____
_____
_____
_____
_____
_____
_____
_____
_____
_____
_____
_____
_____
_____
_____
_____
_____
_____
_____
_____
_____
_____
_____
_____
_____

She makes belted linen garments and sashes to sell the merchants.
-Proverbs 31:24(NLT)

CHAPTER

1	51	101
2	52	102
3	53	103
4	54	104
5	55	105
6	56	106
7	57	107
8	58	108
9	59	109
10	60	110
11	61	111
12	62	112
13	63	113
14	64	114
15	65	115
16	66	116
17	67	117
18	68	118
19	69	119
20	70	120
21	71	121
22	72	122
23	73	123
24	74	124
25	75	125
26	76	126
27	77	127
28	78	128
29	79	129
30	80	130
31	81	131
32	82	132
33	83	133
34	84	134
35	85	135
36	86	136
37	87	137
38	88	138
39	89	139
40	90	140
41	91	141
42	92	142
43	93	143
44	94	144
45	95	145
46	96	146
47	97	147
48	98	148
49	99	149
50	100	150

OLD TESTAMENT

GENESIS EXODUS LEVITICUS NUMBERS
DEUTERONOMY JOSHUA JUDGES RUTH ISAMUEL
IISAMUEL IKINGS IIKINGS ICHRONICLES
IICHRONICLES EZRA NEHEMIAH ESTHER JOB
PSALMS PROVERBS ECCLESIASTES SONG OF
SOLOMON ISAIAH JEREMIAH LAMENTATIONS
EZEKIEL DANIEL HOSEA JOEL AMOS
OBADIAH JONAH MICAH NAHUM HABAKKUK
ZEPHANIAH HAGGAI ZECHARIAH MALACHI

_____
_____
_____
_____
_____
_____
_____
_____
_____
_____
_____
_____

NEW TESTAMENT

MATTHEW MARK LUKE JOHN ACTS ROMANS
ICORINTHIANS IICORINTHIANS GALATIANS
EPHESIANS PHILIPPIANS COLOSSIANS
ITHESSALONIANS IITHESSALONIANS
ITIMOTHY IITIMOTHY TITUS PHILEMON
HEBREWS JAMES IPETER IIPETER IJOHN
IIJOHN IIIJOHN JUDE REVELATION

_____
_____
_____
_____
_____
_____
_____
_____
_____

VERSE

1	51	101	151
2	52	102	152
3	53	103	153
4	54	104	154
5	55	105	155
6	56	106	156
7	57	107	157
8	58	108	158
9	59	109	159
10	60	110	160
11	61	111	161
12	62	112	162
13	63	113	163
14	64	114	164
15	65	115	165
16	66	116	166
17	67	117	167
18	68	118	168
19	69	119	169
20	70	120	170
21	71	121	171
22	72	122	172
23	73	123	173
24	74	124	174
25	75	125	175
26	76	126	176
27	77	127	
28	78	128	
29	79	129	
30	80	130	
31	81	131	
32	82	132	
33	83	133	
34	84	134	
35	85	135	
36	86	136	
37	87	137	
38	88	138	
39	89	139	
40	90	140	
41	91	141	
42	92	142	
43	93	143	
44	94	144	
45	95	145	
46	96	146	
47	97	147	
48	98	148	
49	99	149	
50	100	150	

SPEAKER _____ DATE _____
TOPIC _____ PLACE _____

CHAPTER			OLD TESTAMENT	VERSE			
1	51	101		1	51	101	151
2	52	102	GENESIS EXODUS LEVITICUS NUMBERS	2	52	102	152
3	53	103	DEUTERONOMY JOSHUA JUDGES RUTH ISAMUEL	3	53	103	153
4	54	104	IISAMUEL IKINGS IIKINGS ICHRONICLES	4	54	104	154
5	55	105		5	55	105	155
6	56	106	IICHRONICLES EZRA NEHEMIAH ESTHER JOB	6	56	106	156
7	57	107	PSALMS PROVERBS ECCLESIASTES SONG OF	7	57	107	157
8	58	108	SOLOMON ISAIAH JEREMIAH LAMENTATIONS	8	58	108	158
9	59	109		9	59	109	159
10	60	110	EZEKIEL DANIEL HOSEA JOEL AMOS	10	60	110	160
11	61	111	OBADIAH JONAH MICAH NAHUM HABAKKUK	11	61	111	161
12	62	112	ZEPHANIAH HAGGAI ZECHARIAH MALACHI	12	62	112	162
13	63	113		13	63	113	163
14	64	114		14	64	114	164
15	65	115	_____	15	65	115	165
16	66	116	_____	16	66	116	166
17	67	117	_____	17	67	117	167
18	68	118	_____	18	68	118	168
19	69	119	_____	19	69	119	169
20	70	120	_____	20	70	120	170
21	71	121	_____	21	71	121	171
22	72	122	_____	22	72	122	172
23	73	123	_____	23	73	123	173
24	74	124	_____	24	74	124	174
25	75	125	_____	25	75	125	175
26	76	126	_____	26	76	126	176
27	77	127	_____	27	77	127	
28	78	128	_____	28	78	128	
29	79	129	_____	29	79	129	
30	80	130	_____	30	80	130	
31	81	131	_____	31	81	131	
32	82	132	_____	32	82	132	
33	83	133	_____	33	83	133	
34	84	134	_____	34	84	134	
35	85	135	_____	35	85	135	
36	86	136	_____	36	86	136	
37	87	137		37	87	137	
38	88	138		38	88	138	
39	89	139	**NEW TESTAMENT**	39	89	139	
40	90	140		40	90	140	
41	91	141	MATTHEW MARK LUKE JOHN ACTS ROMANS	41	91	141	
42	92	142	ICORINTHIANS IICORINTHIANS GALATIANS	42	92	142	
43	93	143	EPHESIANS PHILIPPIANS COLOSSIANS	43	93	143	
44	94	144		44	94	144	
45	95	145	ITHESSALONIANS IITHESSALONIANS	45	95	145	
46	96	146	ITIMOTHY IITIMOTHY TITUS PHILEMON	46	96	146	
47	97	147	HEBREWS JAMES IPETER IIPETER IJOHN	47	97	147	
48	98	148		48	98	148	
49	99	149	IIJOHN IIIJOHN JUDE REVELATION	49	99	149	
50	100	150		50	100	150	

NOTES

She is clothed with strength and dignity, and she laughs with no fear of the future.
-Proverbs 31:25 (NLT)

NOTES

When she speaks, her words are wise, and kindness is the rule when she gives instructions.
-Proverbs 31:26(NLT)

REFLECTIONS

_____

_____

_____

_____

_____

_____

_____

_____

_____

_____

_____

_____

_____

_____

_____

_____

_____

_____

_____

_____

_____

_____

_____

_____

_____

_____

_____

_____

*She carefully watches all that goes on in her household and
does not have to bear the consequences of laziness.*
-Proverbs 31:27(NLT)

REFLECTIONS

Her children stand and bless her. Her husband praises her.
-Proverbs 31:28(NLT)

CHAPTER			OLD TESTAMENT	VERSE			
1	51	101		1	51	101	151
2	52	102	GENESIS EXODUS LEVITICUS NUMBERS	2	52	102	152
3	53	103	DEUTERONOMY JOSHUA JUDGES RUTH ISAMUEL	3	53	103	153
4	54	104	IISAMUEL IKINGS IIKINGS ICHRONICLES	4	54	104	154
5	55	105		5	55	105	155
6	56	106	IICHRONICLES EZRA NEHEMIAH ESTHER JOB	6	56	106	156
7	57	107	PSALMS PROVERBS ECCLESIASTES SONG OF	7	57	107	157
8	58	108	SOLOMON ISAIAH JEREMIAH LAMENTATIONS	8	58	108	158
9	59	109		9	59	109	159
10	60	110	EZEKIEL DANIEL HOSEA JOEL AMOS	10	60	110	160
11	61	111	OBADIAH JONAH MICAH NAHUM HABAKKUK	11	61	111	161
12	62	112	ZEPHANIAH HAGGAI ZECHARIAH MALACHI	12	62	112	162
13	63	113		13	63	113	163
14	64	114		14	64	114	164
15	65	115	_____	15	65	115	165
16	66	116	_____	16	66	116	166
17	67	117	_____	17	67	117	167
18	68	118	_____	18	68	118	168
19	69	119	_____	19	69	119	169
20	70	120	_____	20	70	120	170
21	71	121	_____	21	71	121	171
22	72	122	_____	22	72	122	172
23	73	123	_____	23	73	123	173
24	74	124	_____	24	74	124	174
25	75	125	_____	25	75	125	175
26	76	126	_____	26	76	126	176
27	77	127	_____	27	77	127	
28	78	128		28	78	128	
29	79	129	NEW TESTAMENT	29	79	129	
30	80	130		30	80	130	
31	81	131	MATTHEW MARK LUKE JOHN ACTS ROMANS	31	81	131	
32	82	132	ICORINTHIANS IICORINTHIANS GALATIANS	32	82	132	
33	83	133	EPHESIANS PHILIPPIANS COLOSSIANS	33	83	133	
34	84	134		34	84	134	
35	85	135	ITHESSALONIANS IITHESSALONIANS	35	85	135	
36	86	136	ITIMOTHY IITIMOTHY TITUS PHILEMON	36	86	136	
37	87	137	HEBREWS JAMES IPETER IIPETER IJOHN	37	87	137	
38	88	138	IIJOHN IIIJOHN JUDE REVELATION	38	88	138	
39	89	139		39	89	139	
40	90	140		40	90	140	
41	91	141	_____	41	91	141	
42	92	142	_____	42	92	142	
43	93	143	_____	43	93	143	
44	94	144	_____	44	94	144	
45	95	145	_____	45	95	145	
46	96	146	_____	46	96	146	
47	97	147	_____	47	97	147	
48	98	148	_____	48	98	148	
49	99	149	_____	49	99	149	
50	100	150	_____	50	100	150	

CHAPTER			OLD TESTAMENT	VERSE			
1	51	101		1	51	101	151
2	52	102	GENESIS EXODUS LEVITICUS NUMBERS	2	52	102	152
3	53	103	DEUTERONOMY JOSHUA JUDGES RUTH ISAMUEL	3	53	103	153
4	54	104	IISAMUEL IKINGS IIKINGS ICHRONICLES	4	54	104	154
5	55	105		5	55	105	155
6	56	106	IICHRONICLES EZRA NEHEMIAH ESTHER JOB	6	56	106	156
7	57	107	PSALMS PROVERBS ECCLESIASTES SONG OF	7	57	107	157
8	58	108	SOLOMON ISAIAH JEREMIAH LAMENTATIONS	8	58	108	158
9	59	109		9	59	109	159
10	60	110	EZEKIEL DANIEL HOSEA JOEL AMOS	10	60	110	160
11	61	111	OBADIAH JONAH MICAH NAHUM HABAKKUK	11	61	111	161
12	62	112	ZEPHANIAH HAGGAI ZECHARIAH MALACHI	12	62	112	162
13	63	113		13	63	113	163
14	64	114		14	64	114	164
15	65	115	_____	15	65	115	165
16	66	116	_____	16	66	116	166
17	67	117	_____	17	67	117	167
18	68	118	_____	18	68	118	168
19	69	119	_____	19	69	119	169
20	70	120	_____	20	70	120	170
21	71	121	_____	21	71	121	171
22	72	122	_____	22	72	122	172
23	73	123	_____	23	73	123	173
24	74	124	_____	24	74	124	174
25	75	125	_____	25	75	125	175
26	76	126	_____	26	76	126	176
27	77	127	_____	27	77	127	
28	78	128	_____	28	78	128	
29	79	129	_____	29	79	129	
30	80	130	_____	30	80	130	
31	81	131	_____	31	81	131	
32	82	132	_____	32	82	132	
33	83	133	_____	33	83	133	
34	84	134	_____	34	84	134	
35	85	135	_____	35	85	135	
36	86	136	_____	36	86	136	
37	87	137		37	87	137	
38	88	138		38	88	138	
39	89	139	NEW TESTAMENT	39	89	139	
40	90	140		40	90	140	
41	91	141	MATTHEW MARK LUKE JOHN ACTS ROMANS	41	91	141	
42	92	142	ICORINTHIANS IICORINTHIANS GALATIANS	42	92	142	
43	93	143	EPHESIANS PHILIPPIANS COLOSSIANS	43	93	143	
44	94	144		44	94	144	
45	95	145	ITHESSALONIANS IITHESSALONIANS	45	95	145	
46	96	146	ITIMOTHY IITIMOTHY TITUS PHILEMON	46	96	146	
47	97	147	HEBREWS JAMES IPETER IIPETER IJOHN	47	97	147	
48	98	148		48	98	148	
49	99	149	IIJOHN IIIJOHN JUDE REVELATION	49	99	149	
50	100	150		50	100	150	

NOTES

"There are many virtuous and capable women in the world, but you surpass them all!"
-Proverbs 31:29(NLT)

NOTES

_____
_____
_____
_____
_____
_____
_____
_____
_____
_____
_____
_____
_____
_____
_____
_____
_____
_____
_____
_____
_____
_____
_____
_____
_____
_____
_____
_____
_____
_____

Charm is deceptive, and beauty does not last; but a woman
who fears the LORD will be greatly praised.
-Proverbs 31:30(NLT)

REFLECTIONS

_____
_____
_____
_____
_____
_____
_____
_____
_____
_____
_____
_____
_____
_____
_____
_____
_____
_____
_____
_____
_____
_____
_____
_____
_____
_____

Reward her for all she has done. Let her deeds publicly declare her praise.
-Proverbs 31:31(NLT)

REFLECTIONS

An excellent wife, who can find?
For her worth is far above jewels.
-Proverbs 31:10 (NASB)

CHAPTER			**OLD TESTAMENT**	**VERSE**			
1	51	101		1	51	101	151
2	52	102	GENESIS EXODUS LEVITICUS NUMBERS	2	52	102	152
3	53	103	DEUTERONOMY JOSHUA JUDGES RUTH ISAMUEL	3	53	103	153
4	54	104	IISAMUEL IKINGS IIKINGS ICHRONICLES	4	54	104	154
5	55	105	IICHRONICLES EZRA NEHEMIAH ESTHER JOB	5	55	105	155
6	56	106	PSALMS PROVERBS ECCLESIASTES SONG OF	6	56	106	156
7	57	107	SOLOMON ISAIAH JEREMIAH LAMENTATIONS	7	57	107	157
8	58	108	EZEKIEL DANIEL HOSEA JOEL AMOS	8	58	108	158
9	59	109	OBADIAH JONAH MICAH NAHUM HABAKKUK	9	59	109	159
10	60	110	ZEPHANIAH HAGGAI ZECHARIAH MALACHI	10	60	110	160
11	61	111		11	61	111	161
12	62	112		12	62	112	162
13	63	113		13	63	113	163
14	64	114		14	64	114	164
15	65	115	_____	15	65	115	165
16	66	116	_____	16	66	116	166
17	67	117	_____	17	67	117	167
18	68	118	_____	18	68	118	168
19	69	119	_____	19	69	119	169
20	70	120	_____	20	70	120	170
21	71	121	_____	21	71	121	171
22	72	122	_____	22	72	122	172
23	73	123	_____	23	73	123	173
24	74	124	_____	24	74	124	174
25	75	125	_____	25	75	125	175
26	76	126	_____	26	76	126	176
27	77	127	_____	27	77	127	
28	78	128		28	78	128	
29	79	129	**NEW TESTAMENT**	29	79	129	
30	80	130		30	80	130	
31	81	131	MATTHEW MARK LUKE JOHN ACTS ROMANS	31	81	131	
32	82	132	ICORINTHIANS IICORINTHIANS GALATIANS	32	82	132	
33	83	133	EPHESIANS PHILIPPIANS COLOSSIANS	33	83	133	
34	84	134	ITHESSALONIANS IITHESSALONIANS	34	84	134	
35	85	135	ITIMOTHY IITIMOTHY TITUS PHILEMON	35	85	135	
36	86	136	HEBREWS JAMES IPETER IIPETER IJOHN	36	86	136	
37	87	137	IIJOHN IIIJOHN JUDE REVELATION	37	87	137	
38	88	138		38	88	138	
39	89	139		39	89	139	
40	90	140		40	90	140	
41	91	141	_____	41	91	141	
42	92	142	_____	42	92	142	
43	93	143	_____	43	93	143	
44	94	144	_____	44	94	144	
45	95	145	_____	45	95	145	
46	96	146	_____	46	96	146	
47	97	147	_____	47	97	147	
48	98	148	_____	48	98	148	
49	99	149	_____	49	99	149	
50	100	150	_____	50	100	150	

CHAPTER			OLD TESTAMENT	VERSE			
1	51	101		1	51	101	151
2	52	102	GENESIS EXODUS LEVITICUS NUMBERS	2	52	102	152
3	53	103	DEUTERONOMY JOSHUA JUDGES RUTH ISAMUEL	3	53	103	153
4	54	104	IISAMUEL IKINGS IIKINGS ICHRONICLES	4	54	104	154
5	55	105		5	55	105	155
6	56	106	IICHRONICLES EZRA NEHEMIAH ESTHER JOB	6	56	106	156
7	57	107	PSALMS PROVERBS ECCLESIASTES SONG OF	7	57	107	157
8	58	108	SOLOMON ISAIAH JEREMIAH LAMENTATIONS	8	58	108	158
9	59	109		9	59	109	159
10	60	110	EZEKIEL DANIEL HOSEA JOEL AMOS	10	60	110	160
11	61	111	OBADIAH JONAH MICAH NAHUM HABAKKUK	11	61	111	161
12	62	112	ZEPHANIAH HAGGAI ZECHARIAH MALACHI	12	62	112	162
13	63	113		13	63	113	163
14	64	114	_____	14	64	114	164
15	65	115	_____	15	65	115	165
16	66	116	_____	16	66	116	166
17	67	117	_____	17	67	117	167
18	68	118	_____	18	68	118	168
19	69	119	_____	19	69	119	169
20	70	120	_____	20	70	120	170
21	71	121	_____	21	71	121	171
22	72	122	_____	22	72	122	172
23	73	123	_____	23	73	123	173
24	74	124	_____	24	74	124	174
25	75	125	_____	25	75	125	175
26	76	126	_____	26	76	126	176
27	77	127	_____	27	77	127	
28	78	128	_____	28	78	128	
29	79	129	_____	29	79	129	
30	80	130	_____	30	80	130	
31	81	131	_____	31	81	131	
32	82	132	_____	32	82	132	
33	83	133	_____	33	83	133	
34	84	134	_____	34	84	134	
35	85	135	_____	35	85	135	
36	86	136	_____	36	86	136	
37	87	137		37	87	137	
38	88	138		38	88	138	
39	89	139	NEW TESTAMENT	39	89	139	
40	90	140		40	90	140	
41	91	141	MATTHEW MARK LUKE JOHN ACTS ROMANS	41	91	141	
42	92	142	ICORINTHIANS IICORINTHIANS GALATIANS	42	92	142	
43	93	143	EPHESIANS PHILIPPIANS COLOSSIANS	43	93	143	
44	94	144	ITHESSALONIANS IITHESSALONIANS	44	94	144	
45	95	145		45	95	145	
46	96	146	ITIMOTHY IITIMOTHY TITUS PHILEMON	46	96	146	
47	97	147	HEBREWS JAMES IPETER IIPETER IJOHN	47	97	147	
48	98	148	IIJOHN IIIJOHN JUDE REVELATION	48	98	148	
49	99	149		49	99	149	
50	100	150		50	100	150	

NOTES

The heart of her husband trusts in her,
And he will have no lack of gain.
-Proverbs 31:11(NASB)

NOTES

_____
_____
_____
_____
_____
_____
_____
_____
_____
_____
_____
_____
_____
_____
_____
_____
_____
_____
_____
_____
_____
_____
_____
_____
_____
_____
_____
_____
_____

She does him good and not evil
All the days of life.
-Proverbs 31:12(NASB)

REFLECTIONS

She looks for wool and flax
And works with her hands in delight.
-Proverbs 31:13(NASB)

REFLECTIONS

She is like merchant ships;
She brings her food from afar.
-Proverbs 31:14(NASB)

CHAPTER

1	51	101
2	52	102
3	53	103
4	54	104
5	55	105
6	56	106
7	57	107
8	58	108
9	59	109
10	60	110
11	61	111
12	62	112
13	63	113
14	64	114
15	65	115
16	66	116
17	67	117
18	68	118
19	69	119
20	70	120
21	71	121
22	72	122
23	73	123
24	74	124
25	75	125
26	76	126
27	77	127
28	78	128
29	79	129
30	80	130
31	81	131
32	82	132
33	83	133
34	84	134
35	85	135
36	86	136
37	87	137
38	88	138
39	89	139
40	90	140
41	91	141
42	92	142
43	93	143
44	94	144
45	95	145
46	96	146
47	97	147
48	98	148
49	99	149
50	100	150

OLD TESTAMENT

GENESIS EXODUS LEVITICUS NUMBERS
DEUTERONOMY JOSHUA JUDGES RUTH ISAMUEL
IISAMUEL IKINGS IIKINGS ICHRONICLES
IICHRONICLES EZRA NEHEMIAH ESTHER JOB
PSALMS PROVERBS ECCLESIASTES SONG OF
SOLOMON ISAIAH JEREMIAH LAMENTATIONS
EZEKIEL DANIEL HOSEA JOEL AMOS
OBADIAH JONAH MICAH NAHUM HABAKKUK
ZEPHANIAH HAGGAI ZECHARIAH MALACHI

_____
_____
_____
_____
_____
_____
_____
_____
_____
_____
_____
_____
_____

NEW TESTAMENT

MATTHEW MARK LUKE JOHN ACTS ROMANS
ICORINTHIANS IICORINTHIANS GALATIANS
EPHESIANS PHILIPPIANS COLOSSIANS
ITHESSALONIANS IITHESSALONIANS
ITIMOTHY IITIMOTHY TITUS PHILEMON
HEBREWS JAMES IPETER IIPETER IJOHN
IIJOHN IIIJOHN JUDE REVELATION

_____
_____
_____
_____
_____
_____
_____
_____

VERSE

1	51	101	151
2	52	102	152
3	53	103	153
4	54	104	154
5	55	105	155
6	56	106	156
7	57	107	157
8	58	108	158
9	59	109	159
10	60	110	160
11	61	111	161
12	62	112	162
13	63	113	163
14	64	114	164
15	65	115	165
16	66	116	166
17	67	117	167
18	68	118	168
19	69	119	169
20	70	120	170
21	71	121	171
22	72	122	172
23	73	123	173
24	74	124	174
25	75	125	175
26	76	126	176
27	77	127	
28	78	128	
29	79	129	
30	80	130	
31	81	131	
32	82	132	
33	83	133	
34	84	134	
35	85	135	
36	86	136	
37	87	137	
38	88	138	
39	89	139	
40	90	140	
41	91	141	
42	92	142	
43	93	143	
44	94	144	
45	95	145	
46	96	146	
47	97	147	
48	98	148	
49	99	149	
50	100	150	

CHAPTER	OLD TESTAMENT	VERSE

CHAPTER

1	51	101
2	52	102
3	53	103
4	54	104
5	55	105
6	56	106
7	57	107
8	58	108
9	59	109
10	60	110
11	61	111
12	62	112
13	63	113
14	64	114
15	65	115
16	66	116
17	67	117
18	68	118
19	69	119
20	70	120
21	71	121
22	72	122
23	73	123
24	74	124
25	75	125
26	76	126
27	77	127
28	78	128
29	79	129
30	80	130
31	81	131
32	82	132
33	83	133
34	84	134
35	85	135
36	86	136
37	87	137
38	88	138
39	89	139
40	90	140
41	91	141
42	92	142
43	93	143
44	94	144
45	95	145
46	96	146
47	97	147
48	98	148
49	99	149
50	100	150

OLD TESTAMENT

GENESIS EXODUS LEVITICUS NUMBERS
DEUTERONOMY JOSHUA JUDGES RUTH ISAMUEL
IISAMUEL IKINGS IIKINGS ICHRONICLES
IICHRONICLES EZRA NEHEMIAH ESTHER JOB
PSALMS PROVERBS ECCLESIASTES SONG OF
SOLOMON ISAIAH JEREMIAH LAMENTATIONS
EZEKIEL DANIEL HOSEA JOEL AMOS
OBADIAH JONAH MICAH NAHUM HABAKKUK
ZEPHANIAH HAGGAI ZECHARIAH MALACHI

NEW TESTAMENT

MATTHEW MARK LUKE JOHN ACTS ROMANS
ICORINTHIANS IICORINTHIANS GALATIANS
EPHESIANS PHILIPPIANS COLOSSIANS
ITHESSALONIANS IITHESSALONIANS
ITIMOTHY IITIMOTHY TITUS PHILEMON
HEBREWS JAMES IPETER IIPETER IJOHN
IIJOHN IIIJOHN JUDE REVELATION

VERSE

1	51	101	151
2	52	102	152
3	53	103	153
4	54	104	154
5	55	105	155
6	56	106	156
7	57	107	157
8	58	108	158
9	59	109	159
10	60	110	160
11	61	111	161
12	62	112	162
13	63	113	163
14	64	114	164
15	65	115	165
16	66	116	166
17	67	117	167
18	68	118	168
19	69	119	169
20	70	120	170
21	71	121	171
22	72	122	172
23	73	123	173
24	74	124	174
25	75	125	175
26	76	126	176
27	77	127	
28	78	128	
29	79	129	
30	80	130	
31	81	131	
32	82	132	
33	83	133	
34	84	134	
35	85	135	
36	86	136	
37	87	137	
38	88	138	
39	89	139	
40	90	140	
41	91	141	
42	92	142	
43	93	143	
44	94	144	
45	95	145	
46	96	146	
47	97	147	
48	98	148	
49	99	149	
50	100	150	

NOTES

She rises also while it is still night
And gives food to her household
And portions to her maidens.
-Proverbs 31:15(NASB)

NOTES

She considers a field and buys it;
From her earnings she plants a vineyard.
-Proverbs 31:16(NASB)

REFLECTIONS

_____
_____
_____
_____
_____
_____
_____
_____
_____
_____
_____
_____
_____
_____
_____
_____
_____
_____
_____
_____
_____
_____
_____
_____
_____
_____
_____

She girds herself with strength
And makes her arms strong.
-Proverbs 31:17(NASB)

REFLECTIONS

_____

_____

_____

_____

_____

_____

_____

_____

_____

_____

_____

_____

_____

_____

_____

_____

_____

_____

_____

_____

_____

_____

_____

_____

_____

_____

_____

_____

_____

_____

She senses that her gain is good;
Her lamp does not go out at night.
-Proverbs 31:18(NASB)

CHAPTER	OLD TESTAMENT	VERSE

CHAPTER

1	51	101
2	52	102
3	53	103
4	54	104
5	55	105
6	56	106
7	57	107
8	58	108
9	59	109
10	60	110
11	61	111
12	62	112
13	63	113
14	64	114
15	65	115
16	66	116
17	67	117
18	68	118
19	69	119
20	70	120
21	71	121
22	72	122
23	73	123
24	74	124
25	75	125
26	76	126
27	77	127
28	78	128
29	79	129
30	80	130
31	81	131
32	82	132
33	83	133
34	84	134
35	85	135
36	86	136
37	87	137
38	88	138
39	89	139
40	90	140
41	91	141
42	92	142
43	93	143
44	94	144
45	95	145
46	96	146
47	97	147
48	98	148
49	99	149
50	100	150

OLD TESTAMENT

GENESIS EXODUS LEVITICUS NUMBERS
DEUTERONOMY JOSHUA JUDGES RUTH ISAMUEL
IISAMUEL IKINGS IIKINGS ICHRONICLES
IICHRONICLES EZRA NEHEMIAH ESTHER JOB
PSALMS PROVERBS ECCLESIASTES SONG OF
SOLOMON ISAIAH JEREMIAH LAMENTATIONS
EZEKIEL DANIEL HOSEA JOEL AMOS
OBADIAH JONAH MICAH NAHUM HABAKKUK
ZEPHANIAH HAGGAI ZECHARIAH MALACHI

_____
_____
_____
_____
_____
_____
_____
_____
_____
_____
_____
_____

NEW TESTAMENT

MATTHEW MARK LUKE JOHN ACTS ROMANS
ICORINTHIANS IICORINTHIANS GALATIANS
EPHESIANS PHILIPPIANS COLOSSIANS
ITHESSALONIANS IITHESSALONIANS
ITIMOTHY IITIMOTHY TITUS PHILEMON
HEBREWS JAMES IPETER IIPETER IJOHN
IIJOHN IIIJOHN JUDE REVELATION

_____
_____
_____
_____
_____
_____
_____
_____
_____
_____

VERSE

1	51	101	151
2	52	102	152
3	53	103	153
4	54	104	154
5	55	105	155
6	56	106	156
7	57	107	157
8	58	108	158
9	59	109	159
10	60	110	160
11	61	111	161
12	62	112	162
13	63	113	163
14	64	114	164
15	65	115	165
16	66	116	166
17	67	117	167
18	68	118	168
19	69	119	169
20	70	120	170
21	71	121	171
22	72	122	172
23	73	123	173
24	74	124	174
25	75	125	175
26	76	126	176
27	77	127	
28	78	128	
29	79	129	
30	80	130	
31	81	131	
32	82	132	
33	83	133	
34	84	134	
35	85	135	
36	86	136	
37	87	137	
38	88	138	
39	89	139	
40	90	140	
41	91	141	
42	92	142	
43	93	143	
44	94	144	
45	95	145	
46	96	146	
47	97	147	
48	98	148	
49	99	149	
50	100	150	

CHAPTER			OLD TESTAMENT	VERSE			

CHAPTER

1	51	101
2	52	102
3	53	103
4	54	104
5	55	105
6	56	106
7	57	107
8	58	108
9	59	109
10	60	110
11	61	111
12	62	112
13	63	113
14	64	114
15	65	115
16	66	116
17	67	117
18	68	118
19	69	119
20	70	120
21	71	121
22	72	122
23	73	123
24	74	124
25	75	125
26	76	126
27	77	127
28	78	128
29	79	129
30	80	130
31	81	131
32	82	132
33	83	133
34	84	134
35	85	135
36	86	136
37	87	137
38	88	138
39	89	139
40	90	140
41	91	141
42	92	142
43	93	143
44	94	144
45	95	145
46	96	146
47	97	147
48	98	148
49	99	149
50	100	150

OLD TESTAMENT

GENESIS EXODUS LEVITICUS NUMBERS
DEUTERONOMY JOSHUA JUDGES RUTH ISAMUEL
IISAMUEL IKINGS IIKINGS ICHRONICLES
IICHRONICLES EZRA NEHEMIAH ESTHER JOB
PSALMS PROVERBS ECCLESIASTES SONG OF
SOLOMON ISAIAH JEREMIAH LAMENTATIONS
EZEKIEL DANIEL HOSEA JOEL AMOS
OBADIAH JONAH MICAH NAHUM HABAKKUK
ZEPHANIAH HAGGAI ZECHARIAH MALACHI

_____
_____
_____
_____
_____
_____
_____
_____
_____
_____
_____
_____
_____
_____
_____
_____
_____
_____
_____
_____
_____
_____

NEW TESTAMENT

MATTHEW MARK LUKE JOHN ACTS ROMANS
ICORINTHIANS IICORINTHIANS GALATIANS
EPHESIANS PHILIPPIANS COLOSSIANS
ITHESSALONIANS IITHESSALONIANS
ITIMOTHY IITIMOTHY TITUS PHILEMON
HEBREWS JAMES IPETER IIPETER IJOHN
IIJOHN IIIJOHN JUDE REVELATION

VERSE

1	51	101	151
2	52	102	152
3	53	103	153
4	54	104	154
5	55	105	155
6	56	106	156
7	57	107	157
8	58	108	158
9	59	109	159
10	60	110	160
11	61	111	161
12	62	112	162
13	63	113	163
14	64	114	164
15	65	115	165
16	66	116	166
17	67	117	167
18	68	118	168
19	69	119	169
20	70	120	170
21	71	121	171
22	72	122	172
23	73	123	173
24	74	124	174
25	75	125	175
26	76	126	176
27	77	127	
28	78	128	
29	79	129	
30	80	130	
31	81	131	
32	82	132	
33	83	133	
34	84	134	
35	85	135	
36	86	136	
37	87	137	
38	88	138	
39	89	139	
40	90	140	
41	91	141	
42	92	142	
43	93	143	
44	94	144	
45	95	145	
46	96	146	
47	97	147	
48	98	148	
49	99	149	
50	100	150	

NOTES

She stretches out her hands to the distaff,
And her hands grasp the spindle.
-Proverbs 31:19(NASB)

NOTES

She extends her hand to the poor,
And she stretches out her hands to the needy.
-Proverbs 31:20(NASB)

REFLECTIONS

_____
_____
_____
_____
_____
_____
_____
_____
_____
_____
_____
_____
_____
_____
_____
_____
_____
_____
_____
_____
_____
_____
_____
_____
_____
_____
_____
_____

She is not afraid of the snow for her household,
For all her household are clothed with scarlet.
-Proverbs 31:21(NASB)

REFLECTIONS

_____

_____

_____

_____

_____

_____

_____

_____

_____

_____

_____

_____

_____

_____

_____

_____

_____

_____

_____

_____

_____

_____

_____

_____

_____

_____

_____

_____

_____

_____

She makes coverings for herself;
Her clothing is fine linen and purple.
-Proverbs 31:22(NASB)

CHAPTER			OLD TESTAMENT	VERSE			
1	51	101		1	51	101	151
2	52	102	GENESIS EXODUS LEVITICUS NUMBERS	2	52	102	152
3	53	103	DEUTERONOMY JOSHUA JUDGES RUTH ISAMUEL	3	53	103	153
4	54	104	IISAMUEL IKINGS IIKINGS ICHRONICLES	4	54	104	154
5	55	105	IICHRONICLES EZRA NEHEMIAH ESTHER JOB	5	55	105	155
6	56	106	PSALMS PROVERBS ECCLESIASTES SONG OF	6	56	106	156
7	57	107	SOLOMON ISAIAH JEREMIAH LAMENTATIONS	7	57	107	157
8	58	108	EZEKIEL DANIEL HOSEA JOEL AMOS	8	58	108	158
9	59	109	OBADIAH JONAH MICAH NAHUM HABAKKUK	9	59	109	159
10	60	110	ZEPHANIAH HAGGAI ZECHARIAH MALACHI	10	60	110	160
11	61	111		11	61	111	161
12	62	112		12	62	112	162
13	63	113		13	63	113	163
14	64	114	_____	14	64	114	164
15	65	115	_____	15	65	115	165
16	66	116	_____	16	66	116	166
17	67	117	_____	17	67	117	167
18	68	118	_____	18	68	118	168
19	69	119	_____	19	69	119	169
20	70	120	_____	20	70	120	170
21	71	121	_____	21	71	121	171
22	72	122	_____	22	72	122	172
23	73	123	_____	23	73	123	173
24	74	124	_____	24	74	124	174
25	75	125	_____	25	75	125	175
26	76	126	_____	26	76	126	176
27	77	127	_____	27	77	127	
28	78	128		28	78	128	
29	79	129	NEW TESTAMENT	29	79	129	
30	80	130		30	80	130	
31	81	131	MATTHEW MARK LUKE JOHN ACTS ROMANS	31	81	131	
32	82	132	ICORINTHIANS IICORINTHIANS GALATIANS	32	82	132	
33	83	133	EPHESIANS PHILIPPIANS COLOSSIANS	33	83	133	
34	84	134	ITHESSALONIANS IITHESSALONIANS	34	84	134	
35	85	135	ITIMOTHY IITIMOTHY TITUS PHILEMON	35	85	135	
36	86	136	HEBREWS JAMES IPETER IIPETER IJOHN	36	86	136	
37	87	137	IIJOHN IIIJOHN JUDE REVELATION	37	87	137	
38	88	138		38	88	138	
39	89	139		39	89	139	
40	90	140		40	90	140	
41	91	141	_____	41	91	141	
42	92	142	_____	42	92	142	
43	93	143	_____	43	93	143	
44	94	144	_____	44	94	144	
45	95	145	_____	45	95	145	
46	96	146	_____	46	96	146	
47	97	147	_____	47	97	147	
48	98	148	_____	48	98	148	
49	99	149	_____	49	99	149	
50	100	150	_____	50	100	150	

CHAPTER

1	51	101
2	52	102
3	53	103
4	54	104
5	55	105
6	56	106
7	57	107
8	58	108
9	59	109
10	60	110
11	61	111
12	62	112
13	63	113
14	64	114
15	65	115
16	66	116
17	67	117
18	68	118
19	69	119
20	70	120
21	71	121
22	72	122
23	73	123
24	74	124
25	75	125
26	76	126
27	77	127
28	78	128
29	79	129
30	80	130
31	81	131
32	82	132
33	83	133
34	84	134
35	85	135
36	86	136
37	87	137
38	88	138
39	89	139
40	90	140
41	91	141
42	92	142
43	93	143
44	94	144
45	95	145
46	96	146
47	97	147
48	98	148
49	99	149
50	100	150

OLD TESTAMENT

GENESIS EXODUS LEVITICUS NUMBERS
DEUTERONOMY JOSHUA JUDGES RUTH ISAMUEL
IISAMUEL IKINGS IIKINGS ICHRONICLES
IICHRONICLES EZRA NEHEMIAH ESTHER JOB
PSALMS PROVERBS ECCLESIASTES SONG OF
SOLOMON ISAIAH JEREMIAH LAMENTATIONS
EZEKIEL DANIEL HOSEA JOEL AMOS
OBADIAH JONAH MICAH NAHUM HABAKKUK
ZEPHANIAH HAGGAI ZECHARIAH MALACHI

_____
_____
_____
_____
_____
_____
_____
_____
_____
_____
_____
_____
_____
_____
_____
_____
_____
_____
_____
_____
_____
_____

NEW TESTAMENT

MATTHEW MARK LUKE JOHN ACTS ROMANS
ICORINTHIANS IICORINTHIANS GALATIANS
EPHESIANS PHILIPPIANS COLOSSIANS
ITHESSALONIANS IITHESSALONIANS
ITIMOTHY IITIMOTHY TITUS PHILEMON
HEBREWS JAMES IPETER IIPETER IJOHN
IIJOHN IIIJOHN JUDE REVELATION

VERSE

1	51	101	151
2	52	102	152
3	53	103	153
4	54	104	154
5	55	105	155
6	56	106	156
7	57	107	157
8	58	108	158
9	59	109	159
10	60	110	160
11	61	111	161
12	62	112	162
13	63	113	163
14	64	114	164
15	65	115	165
16	66	116	166
17	67	117	167
18	68	118	168
19	69	119	169
20	70	120	170
21	71	121	171
22	72	122	172
23	73	123	173
24	74	124	174
25	75	125	175
26	76	126	176
27	77	127	
28	78	128	
29	79	129	
30	80	130	
31	81	131	
32	82	132	
33	83	133	
34	84	134	
35	85	135	
36	86	136	
37	87	137	
38	88	138	
39	89	139	
40	90	140	
41	91	141	
42	92	142	
43	93	143	
44	94	144	
45	95	145	
46	96	146	
47	97	147	
48	98	148	
49	99	149	
50	100	150	

NOTES

Her husband is known in the gates,
When he sits among the elders of the land.
-Proverbs 31:23(NASB)

NOTES

She makes linen garments and sells **them**,
And supplies belts to the tradesmen.
**-Proverbs 31:24(NASB)**

REFLECTIONS

Strength and dignity are her clothing,
And she smiles at the future.
-Proverbs 31:25(NASB)

REFLECTIONS

She opens her mouth in wisdom,
And the teaching of kindness is on her tongue.
-Proverbs 31:26(NASB)

CHAPTER			OLD TESTAMENT	VERSE			
1	51	101		1	51	101	151
2	52	102	GENESIS EXODUS LEVITICUS NUMBERS	2	52	102	152
3	53	103	DEUTERONOMY JOSHUA JUDGES RUTH ISAMUEL	3	53	103	153
4	54	104	IISAMUEL IKINGS IIKINGS ICHRONICLES	4	54	104	154
5	55	105	IICHRONICLES EZRA NEHEMIAH ESTHER JOB	5	55	105	155
6	56	106	PSALMS PROVERBS ECCLESIASTES SONG OF	6	56	106	156
7	57	107	SOLOMON ISAIAH JEREMIAH LAMENTATIONS	7	57	107	157
8	58	108	EZEKIEL DANIEL HOSEA JOEL AMOS	8	58	108	158
9	59	109	OBADIAH JONAH MICAH NAHUM HABAKKUK	9	59	109	159
10	60	110	ZEPHANIAH HAGGAI ZECHARIAH MALACHI	10	60	110	160
11	61	111		11	61	111	161
12	62	112		12	62	112	162
13	63	113		13	63	113	163
14	64	114	_____	14	64	114	164
15	65	115	_____	15	65	115	165
16	66	116	_____	16	66	116	166
17	67	117	_____	17	67	117	167
18	68	118	_____	18	68	118	168
19	69	119	_____	19	69	119	169
20	70	120	_____	20	70	120	170
21	71	121	_____	21	71	121	171
22	72	122	_____	22	72	122	172
23	73	123	_____	23	73	123	173
24	74	124	_____	24	74	124	174
25	75	125	_____	25	75	125	175
26	76	126	_____	26	76	126	176
27	77	127	_____	27	77	127	
28	78	128		28	78	128	
29	79	129	NEW TESTAMENT	29	79	129	
30	80	130		30	80	130	
31	81	131	MATTHEW MARK LUKE JOHN ACTS ROMANS	31	81	131	
32	82	132	ICORINTHIANS IICORINTHIANS GALATIANS	32	82	132	
33	83	133	EPHESIANS PHILIPPIANS COLOSSIANS	33	83	133	
34	84	134	ITHESSALONIANS IITHESSALONIANS	34	84	134	
35	85	135	ITIMOTHY IITIMOTHY TITUS PHILEMON	35	85	135	
36	86	136	HEBREWS JAMES IPETER IIPETER IJOHN	36	86	136	
37	87	137	IIJOHN IIIJOHN JUDE REVELATION	37	87	137	
38	88	138		38	88	138	
39	89	139		39	89	139	
40	90	140		40	90	140	
41	91	141	_____	41	91	141	
42	92	142	_____	42	92	142	
43	93	143	_____	43	93	143	
44	94	144	_____	44	94	144	
45	95	145	_____	45	95	145	
46	96	146	_____	46	96	146	
47	97	147	_____	47	97	147	
48	98	148	_____	48	98	148	
49	99	149	_____	49	99	149	
50	100	150	_____	50	100	150	

CHAPTER

1	51	101
2	52	102
3	53	103
4	54	104
5	55	105
6	56	106
7	57	107
8	58	108
9	59	109
10	60	110
11	61	111
12	62	112
13	63	113
14	64	114
15	65	115
16	66	116
17	67	117
18	68	118
19	69	119
20	70	120
21	71	121
22	72	122
23	73	123
24	74	124
25	75	125
26	76	126
27	77	127
28	78	128
29	79	129
30	80	130
31	81	131
32	82	132
33	83	133
34	84	134
35	85	135
36	86	136
37	87	137
38	88	138
39	89	139
40	90	140
41	91	141
42	92	142
43	93	143
44	94	144
45	95	145
46	96	146
47	97	147
48	98	148
49	99	149
50	100	150

OLD TESTAMENT

GENESIS EXODUS LEVITICUS NUMBERS
DEUTERONOMY JOSHUA JUDGES RUTH ISAMUEL
IISAMUEL IKINGS IIKINGS ICHRONICLES
IICHRONICLES EZRA NEHEMIAH ESTHER JOB
PSALMS PROVERBS ECCLESIASTES SONG OF
SOLOMON ISAIAH JEREMIAH LAMENTATIONS
EZEKIEL DANIEL HOSEA JOEL AMOS
OBADIAH JONAH MICAH NAHUM HABAKKUK
ZEPHANIAH HAGGAI ZECHARIAH MALACHI

_____
_____
_____
_____
_____
_____
_____
_____
_____
_____
_____
_____
_____
_____
_____
_____
_____
_____
_____
_____
_____

NEW TESTAMENT

MATTHEW MARK LUKE JOHN ACTS ROMANS
ICORINTHIANS IICORINTHIANS GALATIANS
EPHESIANS PHILIPPIANS COLOSSIANS
ITHESSALONIANS IITHESSALONIANS
ITIMOTHY IITIMOTHY TITUS PHILEMON
HEBREWS JAMES IPETER IIPETER IJOHN
IIJOHN IIIJOHN JUDE REVELATION

VERSE

1	51	101	151
2	52	102	152
3	53	103	153
4	54	104	154
5	55	105	155
6	56	106	156
7	57	107	157
8	58	108	158
9	59	109	159
10	60	110	160
11	61	111	161
12	62	112	162
13	63	113	163
14	64	114	164
15	65	115	165
16	66	116	166
17	67	117	167
18	68	118	168
19	69	119	169
20	70	120	170
21	71	121	171
22	72	122	172
23	73	123	173
24	74	124	174
25	75	125	175
26	76	126	176
27	77	127	
28	78	128	
29	79	129	
30	80	130	
31	81	131	
32	82	132	
33	83	133	
34	84	134	
35	85	135	
36	86	136	
37	87	137	
38	88	138	
39	89	139	
40	90	140	
41	91	141	
42	92	142	
43	93	143	
44	94	144	
45	95	145	
46	96	146	
47	97	147	
48	98	148	
49	99	149	
50	100	150	

NOTES

She looks well to the ways of her household,
And does not eat the bread of idleness.
-Proverbs 31:27(NASB)

NOTES

Her children rise up and bless her;
Her husband **also**, and he praises her, **saying:**
**-Proverbs 31:28(NASB)**

REFLECTIONS

"Many daughters have done nobly,
But you excel them all."
-Proverbs 31:29 (NASB)

REFLECTIONS

Charm is deceitful and beauty is vain,
But _a woman who fears the LORD, she shall be praised._
-Proverbs 31:30(NASB)

CHAPTER			OLD TESTAMENT	VERSE			

CHAPTER

			OLD TESTAMENT		VERSE		
1	51	101		1	51	101	151
2	52	102	GENESIS EXODUS LEVITICUS NUMBERS	2	52	102	152
3	53	103	DEUTERONOMY JOSHUA JUDGES RUTH ISAMUEL	3	53	103	153
4	54	104	IISAMUEL IKINGS IIKINGS ICHRONICLES	4	54	104	154
5	55	105	IICHRONICLES EZRA NEHEMIAH ESTHER JOB	5	55	105	155
6	56	106	PSALMS PROVERBS ECCLESIASTES SONG OF	6	56	106	156
7	57	107	SOLOMON ISAIAH JEREMIAH LAMENTATIONS	7	57	107	157
8	58	108	EZEKIEL DANIEL HOSEA JOEL AMOS	8	58	108	158
9	59	109	OBADIAH JONAH MICAH NAHUM HABAKKUK	9	59	109	159
10	60	110	ZEPHANIAH HAGGAI ZECHARIAH MALACHI	10	60	110	160
11	61	111		11	61	111	161
12	62	112		12	62	112	162
13	63	113		13	63	113	163
14	64	114		14	64	114	164
15	65	115	_____	15	65	115	165
16	66	116	_____	16	66	116	166
17	67	117	_____	17	67	117	167
18	68	118	_____	18	68	118	168
19	69	119	_____	19	69	119	169
20	70	120	_____	20	70	120	170
21	71	121	_____	21	71	121	171
22	72	122	_____	22	72	122	172
23	73	123	_____	23	73	123	173
24	74	124	_____	24	74	124	174
25	75	125	_____	25	75	125	175
26	76	126	_____	26	76	126	176
27	77	127	_____	27	77	127	
28	78	128		28	78	128	
29	79	129	NEW TESTAMENT	29	79	129	
30	80	130		30	80	130	
31	81	131	MATTHEW MARK LUKE JOHN ACTS ROMANS	31	81	131	
32	82	132	ICORINTHIANS IICORINTHIANS GALATIANS	32	82	132	
33	83	133	EPHESIANS PHILIPPIANS COLOSSIANS	33	83	133	
34	84	134	ITHESSALONIANS IITHESSALONIANS	34	84	134	
35	85	135	ITIMOTHY IITIMOTHY TITUS PHILEMON	35	85	135	
36	86	136	HEBREWS JAMES IPETER IIPETER IJOHN	36	86	136	
37	87	137	IIJOHN IIIJOHN JUDE REVELATION	37	87	137	
38	88	138		38	88	138	
39	89	139		39	89	139	
40	90	140		40	90	140	
41	91	141	_____	41	91	141	
42	92	142	_____	42	92	142	
43	93	143	_____	43	93	143	
44	94	144	_____	44	94	144	
45	95	145	_____	45	95	145	
46	96	146	_____	46	96	146	
47	97	147	_____	47	97	147	
48	98	148	_____	48	98	148	
49	99	149	_____	49	99	149	
50	100	150	_____	50	100	150	

SPEAKER _____ DATE _____
TOPIC _____ PLACE _____

CHAPTER

1	51	101
2	52	102
3	53	103
4	54	104
5	55	105
6	56	106
7	57	107
8	58	108
9	59	109
10	60	110
11	61	111
12	62	112
13	63	113
14	64	114
15	65	115
16	66	116
17	67	117
18	68	118
19	69	119
20	70	120
21	71	121
22	72	122
23	73	123
24	74	124
25	75	125
26	76	126
27	77	127
28	78	128
29	79	129
30	80	130
31	81	131
32	82	132
33	83	133
34	84	134
35	85	135
36	86	136
37	87	137
38	88	138
39	89	139
40	90	140
41	91	141
42	92	142
43	93	143
44	94	144
45	95	145
46	96	146
47	97	147
48	98	148
49	99	149
50	100	150

OLD TESTAMENT

GENESIS EXODUS LEVITICUS NUMBERS
DEUTERONOMY JOSHUA JUDGES RUTH ISAMUEL
IISAMUEL IKINGS IIKINGS ICHRONICLES
IICHRONICLES EZRA NEHEMIAH ESTHER JOB
PSALMS PROVERBS ECCLESIASTES SONG OF
SOLOMON ISAIAH JEREMIAH LAMENTATIONS
EZEKIEL DANIEL HOSEA JOEL AMOS
OBADIAH JONAH MICAH NAHUM HABAKKUK
ZEPHANIAH HAGGAI ZECHARIAH MALACHI

_____
_____
_____
_____
_____
_____
_____
_____
_____
_____
_____
_____
_____
_____
_____
_____
_____
_____
_____
_____
_____

NEW TESTAMENT

MATTHEW MARK LUKE JOHN ACTS ROMANS
ICORINTHIANS IICORINTHIANS GALATIANS
EPHESIANS PHILIPPIANS COLOSSIANS
ITHESSALONIANS IITHESSALONIANS
ITIMOTHY IITIMOTHY TITUS PHILEMON
HEBREWS JAMES IPETER IIPETER IJOHN
IIJOHN IIIJOHN JUDE REVELATION

VERSE

1	51	101	151
2	52	102	152
3	53	103	153
4	54	104	154
5	55	105	155
6	56	106	156
7	57	107	157
8	58	108	158
9	59	109	159
10	60	110	160
11	61	111	161
12	62	112	162
13	63	113	163
14	64	114	164
15	65	115	165
16	66	116	166
17	67	117	167
18	68	118	168
19	69	119	169
20	70	120	170
21	71	121	171
22	72	122	172
23	73	123	173
24	74	124	174
25	75	125	175
26	76	126	176
27	77	127	
28	78	128	
29	79	129	
30	80	130	
31	81	131	
32	82	132	
33	83	133	
34	84	134	
35	85	135	
36	86	136	
37	87	137	
38	88	138	
39	89	139	
40	90	140	
41	91	141	
42	92	142	
43	93	143	
44	94	144	
45	95	145	
46	96	146	
47	97	147	
48	98	148	
49	99	149	
50	100	150	

NOTES

_____
_____
_____
_____
_____
_____
_____
_____
_____
_____
_____
_____
_____
_____
_____
_____
_____
_____
_____
_____
_____
_____
_____
_____
_____
_____
_____
_____
_____
_____

Give her the product of her hands,
And let her works praise her in the gates.
-Proverbs 31:31(NASB)

NOTES

But they that wait upon the LORD shall renew their strength; they shall mount up with wings as eagles; they shall run, and not be weary; and they shall walk and not faint.
-Isaiah 40:31 (KJV)

REFLECTIONS

_____
_____
_____
_____
_____
_____
_____
_____
_____
_____
_____
_____
_____
_____
_____
_____
_____
_____
_____
_____
_____
_____
_____
_____
_____
_____
_____
_____
_____
_____

But ye, beloved, building up yourselves on your most holy faith, praying in the Holy Ghost.
-Jude 1:20 (KJV)

REFLECTIONS

I can do all things through Christ which strengtheneth me.
-Philippians 4:13 (KJV)

EVENTS

JANUARY

_____

_____

_____

MARCH

_____

_____

_____

MAY

_____

_____

_____

JULY

_____

_____

_____

SEPTEMBER

_____

_____

_____

NOVEMBER

_____

_____

_____

FEBRUARY

_____

_____

_____

APRIL

_____

_____

_____

JUNE

_____

_____

_____

AUGUST

_____

_____

_____

OCTOBER

_____

_____

_____

DECEMBER

_____

_____

_____

ADDRESS

Name _____
Address _____
_____
_____
Phone # _____
E-Mail _____

Name _____
Address _____
_____
_____
Phone # _____
E-Mail _____

Name _____
Address _____
_____
_____
Phone # _____
E-Mail _____

Name _____
Address _____
_____
_____
Phone # _____
E-Mail _____

Name _____
Address _____
_____
_____
Phone # _____
E-Mail _____

Name _____
Address _____
_____
_____
Phone # _____
E-Mail _____

Name _____
Address _____
_____
_____
Phone # _____
E-Mail _____

Name _____
Address _____
_____
_____
Phone # _____
E-Mail _____

Name
Address

Phone #
E-Mail

Name
Address

Phone #
E-Mail

Name
Address

Phone #
E-Mail

Name
Address

Phone #
E-Mail

Name
Address

Phone #
E-Mail

Name
Address

Phone #
E-Mail